VOCABULARY

HISTORY AND GEOGRAPHY WORDS

- ♦ Historic Turning Points
- ♦ Leaders Then and Now
- ♦ See the USA
- ♦ Wonders of the World

JOANNE SUTER

EVERYDAY LIVING WORDS

HISTORY AND GEOGRAPHY WORDS

MEDIA AND MARKETPLACE WORDS

MUSIC, ART, AND LITERATURE WORDS

SCIENCE AND TECHNOLOGY WORDS

WORKPLACE AND CAREER WORDS

SADDLEBACK
EDUCATIONAL PUBLISHING
Three Watson,
Irvine, CA 92618-2767,
Website: www.sdlback.com

Development and Production: Laurel Associates, Inc.
Cover Design: Elisa Ligon
Interior Illustrations: Katherine Urrutia, Debra A. LaPalm, C.S. Arts

ISBN-13: 978-1-56254-394-5
ISBN-10: 1-56254-394-6
eBook: 978-1-60291-478-0

Printed in the United States of America
12 11 10 09 08 9 8 7 6 5 4 3 2

CONTENTS

INTRODUCTION

Welcome to VOCABULARY IN CONTEXT!

A well-developed vocabulary pays off in many important ways. Better-than-average "word power" makes it easier to understand everything you read and hear—from textbook assignments to TV news reports or instructions on how to repair a bicycle. And word power obviously increases your effectiveness as a communicator. Think about it: *As far as other people are concerned, your ideas are only as convincing as the words you use to express them.* In other words, the vocabulary you use when you speak or write always significantly adds or detracts from what you have to say.

VOCABULARY IN CONTEXT was written especially for *you*. The program was designed to enrich your personal "word bank" with many hundreds of high-frequency and challenging words. There are six thematic books in the series—**Everyday Living Words**, **Workplace and Career Words**, **Science and Technology Words**, **Media and Marketplace Words**, **History and Geography Words**, and **Music, Art, and Literature Words**. Each worktext presents topic-related readings with key terms in context. Follow-up exercises provide a wide variety of practice activities to help you unlock the meanings of unfamiliar words. These strategies include the study of synonyms and antonyms; grammatical word forms; word roots, prefixes, and suffixes; connotations; and the efficient use of a dictionary and thesaurus. Thinking skills, such as drawing conclusions and completing analogies, are included as reinforcement.

A word of advice: Don't stop "thinking about words" when you finish this program. A first-class vocabulary must be constantly renewed! In order to earn a reputation as a first-rate communicator, you must incorporate the new words you learn into your everyday speech and writing.

UNIT 1

PREVIEW

Test your knowledge of the vocabulary skills, concepts, and terms you will study in this unit. Answers are upside down on the bottom of the page.

TRUE OR FALSE?

Write **T** or **F** to show whether each statement is *true* or *false*.

1. _____ A *democracy* is usually headed by a *tyrant*.

2. _____ *Eighty degrees* can also be written *80°*.

3. _____ The words *climate* and *weather* are antonyms.

4. _____ The words *boundaries* and *borders* are synonyms.

5. _____ The adjective form of *patriot* is *patriotic*.

6. _____ A *civil war* is fought between a country and its overseas colonies.

7. _____ *Battlefield, freedom,* and *bloodshed* are all compound words.

8. _____ In the word *midnight*, the suffix *mid-* means "in the middle of."

SPELLING

Circle the correctly spelled word in each group.

1. colunist   collonist   colonist

2. empiror   emperor   emperer

3. Massachusetts   massachusetts   Masachusetes

4. goverment   govarment   government

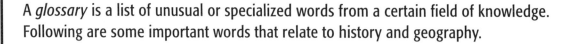

GLOSSARY

A *glossary* is a list of unusual or specialized words from a certain field of knowledge. Following are some important words that relate to history and geography.

canyon a long, narrow valley with high cliffs on each side, often with a stream running through it

civil war war between sections or groups of people of the same nation

climate the average weather conditions in a certain region over a period of years

coast land along the sea

colonist one of a group of people who settle in a distant land, but remain under the rule of the home country

czar the title of any of the former emperors of Russia

democracy government in which the people hold the ruling power

empire a group of countries or territories under the rule of one government or person

jungle a tropical land thickly covered with trees and other plants and usually filled with animals

longitude distance measured in degrees east and west of an imaginary line running from the North Pole to the South Pole

North Pole the spot that is farthest north on the Earth

patriot a person who shows great love and loyalty toward his or her own country

prime meridian the imaginary line from which longitude is measured both east and west. Located at 0° longitude, it passes through Greenwich, England.

regent a person chosen to rule while a king or queen is absent, sick, or too young to take the throne

serfs farm workers who, almost like slaves, belong to a landowner

South Pole the spot that is farthest south on the Earth

terrain ground or area of land

tyrant a cruel or unjust ruler who has complete power

VOCABULARY IN CONTEXT

Complete each sentence with a word from the glossary. Use the other words in the sentence to help you decide which word to add. Check the dictionary definition if you're still not sure.

1. Year after year, the flowing river made the _____ deeper.

2. The ruler was a power-hungry _____ who demanded total control of his people.

3. The rocky, uneven _____ made travel by vehicle impossible.

4. Because the new king was only 10 years old, a _____ would head the government for several years.

5. When powerful families from two different regions claimed power, _____ broke out.

6. Around the whole Earth, there are 360° of _____.

7. The nobleman was a wealthy landowner who had many _____ farming his lands.

WORD FORMS

Add vowels (a, e, i, o, u) to complete a different form of some words from the glossary. Use context clues to help.

1. Pollutants in the air can cause a cl__m__t__c change in a region.

2. The __mp__r__r ruled his vast lands from the capital city.

3. C__ __st__l winds often bring rain from the west.

4. He felt it was his p__tr__ __t__c duty to vote in every election.

5. Massachusetts was one of the 13 original c__l__n__ __s.

6. P__l__r explorers found conditions unlike anywhere else on Earth.

SCRAMBLED WORDS

First unscramble the words from the glossary. Then solve the crossword puzzle with words that complete the sentences.

NOOLTISC _____   MEIRPE _____

GLUNJE _____   CAMECYDRO _____

LICTAME _____   ZRAC _____

ACROSS

3. Although living across the sea, every American ____ had to follow the laws of England.

5. The arctic ____ is so cold that some lakes never thaw.

6. For nearly 20 years, the ____ ruled all of Russia.

DOWN

1. Huge vines hung from the trees in the hot, steamy ____.

2. The founding fathers of the United States wanted a ____ in which every citizen had a voice in government.

4. The ruler added to his ____ by conquering many small tribes.

WORD HISTORY

Some glossary words have origins in other languages. Write a letter to match each **boldface** word with its origin. If necessary, check a dictionary.

1. _____ **canyon**

2. _____ **czar**

3. _____ **democracy**

4. _____ **empire**

5. _____ **serf**

6. _____ **terrain**

a. from the Latin word *caesar*, meaning "emperor"

b. from the Latin word *servus*, meaning "slave"

c. from ancient Greek words meaning "the people" and "to rule"

d. from the Latin word *imperium*, meaning "command, authority, realm"

e. from the Spanish word *cañon*, meaning "a pipe," "a tube," or "a gorge"

f. from the French word *terra*, meaning "earth"

8

Time Zones

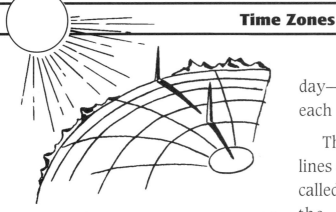

"Good morning," Maria said when she telephoned her cousin Sam in New York. "It's already a balmy Saturday here in California!"

"Good *morning?*" her cousin laughed. "Are you kidding? I'm just about to eat lunch!"

Maria had forgotten all about the three-hour time difference between the west and east coasts of the United States. When it is 9:00 A.M. in California, it is 12:00 noon in New York.

There is a geographical reason why clocks in different parts of the world show different times. Time is measured by the sun. As the Earth rotates, the sun shines on different parts of it. The side of the Earth facing the sun experiences daytime while the side turned away from the sun experiences night. Every 24 hours, the Earth completes a rotation. That means there are 24 hours in a day—and there is a time zone for each one of those hours.

The time zones closely follow the lines of longitude. An imaginary line called the *prime meridian* goes from the North Pole to the South Pole. It passes through Greenwich, England and is the starting point for measuring longitude. Longitude is measured in degrees, so the prime meridian has been designated 0° longitude. There are 12 time zones east of the prime meridian and 12 west of it. Another imaginary line, called the International Date Line, marks 180° longitude—halfway around the Earth. When it is noon at the prime meridian, it is midnight at 180° longitude.

The United States has eight standard time zones. The time in each zone is one hour different from its neighboring zones. To the west of each zone, times are earlier. To the east of each zone, times are later. Sam lives on Eastern Standard Time. Maria lives on Pacific Standard Time—three time zones to the west. That's why it is 9:00 for her when it is noon for Sam.

WORD SEARCH

1. What 12-letter adjective from the reading means "having to do with the study of the Earth's surface and natural features"? *g*_____

2. What four-letter noun from the reading means "an area or region that is set apart from the parts around it in some special way"? *z*_____

3. What nine-letter noun means "a distance east and west measured by an imaginary line running from the North Pole to the South Pole"? *l*_____

4. What two words name a line of longitude that is measured as 0°? *p*_____ *m*_____

5. What names are given to the spots that are farthest north and south on Earth? *N*_____ *P*_____ and *S*_____ *P*_____

ANALOGIES

Analogies are statements of relationship. To come up with the missing word, you must figure out the relationship between the first two words. Then complete each analogy with a word from the reading that shows the same relationship.

1. *East coast* is to *west coast* as *North Pole* is to *S*_____ *P*_____.

2. *Lines of latitude* are to *horizontal* as *lines of l*_____ are to *vertical*.

3. *Everything* is to *nothing* as *nighttime* is to *d*_____.

4. *Breakfast* is to *morning* as *l*_____ is to *noon*.

5. *Plus* is to *+* as *degree* is to _____.

EASILY CONFUSED WORDS

Circle the word that correctly completes each sentence.

1. When (it's / its) 3:00 P.M. in Oregon, it is 6:00 P.M. in New York.

2. The Earth never stops rotating on (it's / its) axis.

3. "I'm (already / all ready) eating lunch!" exclaimed Sam.

4. The seven travelers were (already / all ready) to board the airplane.

SYNONYMS

Complete the puzzle with words from the reading. Clue word are *synonyms* (words with a similar meaning) of the answer words.

ACROSS

4. warm

5. 12:00 P.M.

7. bordering

8. cipher

DOWN

1. midpoint

2. 12:00 A.M.

3. unreal

6. turn

(Crossword puzzle grid with numbered cells: 1-H, 2-M, 3-I, 4-B, 5-N, 6-R, 7-N, 8-Z)

MULTIPLE-MEANING WORDS

Many words have different meanings, depending on their context. Read the two definitions of each word. Then circle a letter to show the meaning *used in the reading*. Finally, use that meaning of the word in a sentence of your own.

1. a. **coast:** land along the sea   b. **coast:** to slide downhill

   YOUR SENTENCE: _____

2. a. **Earth:** the planet we live on   b. **earth:** soil or ground

   YOUR SENTENCE: _____

3. a. **degrees:** units used to measure temperature

   b. **degrees:** units used to measure angles and arcs of circles

   YOUR SENTENCE: _____

4. a. **standard:** something set up as a model to use for comparison

   b. **standard:** a flag or banner of a military group or government

   YOUR SENTENCE: _____

The Remarkable Road of the Inca Empire

Throughout the 15th century and into the 16th, a mighty empire thrived along the west coast of South America. This was the land of the Inca. It was ruled by an emperor believed to be the son of the sun god. This godly mortal, known as the Sapa Inca, faced a daunting job. He needed to figure out a way to unite his vast lands and many peoples.

The emperor decided to link the parts of his empire with an amazing system of roads. This was a time when most European roads were dirt tracks. Eventually, the Inca roads covered 12,000 miles of desert and mountains. Builders stretched bridges across rivers and canyons. They cut tunnels through mountains and chiseled steps into slopes. The incredible Inca engineers tackled varied climates and terrain—from steep, icy mountain sides to windswept lowlands and steaming jungles.

The Royal Road of the Inca may well be the world's greatest feat of engineering. It ran more than 1,250 miles—between the capital, Cuzco, and the city of Quito in the north of the empire. For most of its length, the roadway was arrow-straight and 24 feet wide. The paving stones fit tightly together like pieces of a jigsaw puzzle. Trees gave shade, and a stream flowing in a roadside ditch provided water.

The Inca road system was off-limits to commoners—farmers or crafts people, for example. Regular travelers included the Sapa Inca's warriors and messengers. Relay teams carried news throughout the empire. They had to memorize their messages. Why? Because the Inca had no system of written language. A message could travel the 1,250 miles from Quito to Cuzco in five days. Travelers journeyed the Royal Road by foot—perhaps accompanied by a llama to carry gear. Despite their engineering genius, the Incas had not invented the wheel!

WORD SEARCH

1. What seven-letter plural noun from the reading means "long, narrow valleys with high cliffs on each side"?

   c _____

2. What seven-letter noun from the reading means "the usual patterns of weather conditions in a certain place"?

c _____

3. What seven-letter noun from the reading means "the ground, or an area of land"?

t _____

4. What five-letter adjective from the reading describes an event in which each member of a team runs only a certain part of the whole distance?

r _____

SYNONYMS

Complete the puzzle with words from the reading. Clue words are *synonyms* (words with a similar meaning) of the answer words.

ACROSS

1. remarkable, amazing

4. prospered, flourished

5. human

6. fearsome, dismaying

DOWN

2. carved

3. trench, channel

HOMONYMS

Homonyms are words that sound the same but have different spellings and meanings. For example, the words *bear* (the animal) and *bare* (without covering) are homonyms. Circle the correct homonym in each sentence below.

1. The Royal Road was 1,250 (feat / feet) long.

2. The Inca believed their emperor was the (sun / son) of a god.

3. The Inca worshipped the (sun / son), which gave them light and warmth.

terrain   Artisan   Climate

4. The Inca had amazing roads, but they had not invented the (wheel / we'll).

5. Cuzco was the (capital / capitol) city of the empire.

6. Each stone fit together like a (piece / peace) of a jigsaw puzzle.

COMPOUND WORDS

Write a compound word from the reading to complete each sentence.

1. Artisans who craft tools and goods are called _____.

2. An area that is banned or forbidden is said to be _____.

3. A paved surface used for travel is called a _____.

4. The land bordering a traveler's route may be called the

   _____.

5. _____ are regions that are lower than the land around them.

SUFFIXES MEANING "ONE WHO"

Words that end in *-or, -er,* or *-eer* often name people, such as *doctors, hikers,* and *pioneers,* who "do something." Complete each sentence with a word from the reading that ends with one of these suffixes. Check a dictionary if you need help.

1. An _____ plans and designs roads, bridges, buildings, and such.

2. A _____ erects buildings and other structures.

3. A _____ tills the soil before planting, growing, and harvesting crops.

4. One who journeys from place to place is a _____.

5. In all ages and places, _____ fight in wars.

Czar Peter the Great

In the 17th century, two boys were ready to inherit the throne of Russia. The czar had died, and his grandsons—Ivan and Peter—were next in line to rule. Since both were young, their sister Sophia served as regent.

Peter spent his youth in the countryside. There, the ambitious, energetic boy launched an old boat and learned to sail. As a teenager he lived in the capital city of Moscow. Its residents and their European clothing and food were fascinating to the boy from the country.

Peter grew to be a giant of a man—nearly seven feet tall! By age 17, he knew that he wanted the throne. He forced his sister Sophia to resign. Ten years later, his brother Ivan died. Peter became sole ruler of Russia, a country that had become the largest in the world. Russia had, however, kept itself isolated. It had fallen far behind the West in science and education. Peter planned to change that in a big way.

Setting sail for Europe, he became the first Russian czar to travel overseas. When Czar Peter returned to Russia, he brought weapons and scientific tools. He also brought artisans, engineers, and soldiers to teach his people European skills. Two barbers were included in the group. Why? Peter had decided that his noblemen must adopt western fashions. He ordered them to shave their long beards and get rid of their flowing robes. Russian subjects did as Peter ordered. They knew their czar was a tyrant with a bad temper! He could be very cruel to anyone who did not agree with him.

Czar Peter built the city of St. Petersburg. It would replace Moscow as the capital. He called the European-styled city his "Window on the West" and declared that it would open Russia to the world. Then Peter claimed a new title. He became *Peter the Great, Emperor and Father of the Fatherland.*

With his European-style reforms, Peter brought Russia into the modern age. He extended its borders and power. Still, most Russians remained poor serfs, tied to the land of the nobles they served. Peter's "great" reforms did nothing to improve the lives of the masses.

WORD SEARCH

1. What nine-letter verb from the reading means "got something from a relative when that person died"?

   *i*_____

2. What nine-letter adjective from the reading means "having a strong desire to gain fame, power, or wealth"?

   *a*_____

3. What seven-letter plural noun from the reading means "changes meant to improve the ways things are at present"?

   *r*_____

COMPOUND WORDS

First unscramble the *compound words* (one word made from two or more words) from the reading. Then use each unscrambled word to complete one of the sentences.

SADROGSNN _____	**VASOERSE** _____
HEFTANLARD _____	**YESDOCTUNIR** _____

1. Russian people referred to their country as the _____.

2. When the old czar died, his two _____ were still very young.

3. Peter was the first czar to travel _____ to Europe.

4. Peter spent his younger years in the Russian _____.

HOMONYMS

Homonyms are words that sound the same but are spelled differently and have different meanings. In each sentence below, a homonym is used incorrectly. Circle the error. Then write the correct homonym on the line. The first one has been done for you.

1. Peter became the (soul) ruler of Russia.   *sole*_____

2. The Russian surfs, who worked the land, remained poor and powerless under Peter's rule.   _____

3. Peter claimed the Russian thrown when he was 17 years old.   _____

4. As a young boy, Peter learned to sale a boat.   _____

5. Peter the Great brought knew tools and
    styles from Europe.   _____

WORD MEANINGS

Complete the puzzle with words from the
reading. Clues are **boldface** words in the sentences.

ACROSS

1. Peter built St. Petersburg to be the
    new Russian **seat of government**.

3. Peter ordered every noble to
    get rid of his **chin hairs.**

6. Peter was so tall people called him a
    person of unusually huge stature.

DOWN

2. Peter claimed a new **name showing
    rank or role**, calling himself "Peter
    the Great."

3. Peter brought home two **hair stylists**
    to spread western fashion.

4. Sophia, Peter's sister, was forced to
    give up her job as acting ruler of Russia.

5. Czar Peter was known
    as the **male parent** of
    the Fatherland.

Puzzle grid — Across: 1 (C ... 2), 3 (B ... 4 R), 6 (G); Down: 2 (T), 5 (F)

WHO ARE THEY?

Match each word in the first column with the type of person it names. Write a letter
by each number.

1. _____ **czar**

2. _____ **regent**

3. _____ **artisan**

4. _____ **serf**

5. _____ **subjects**

a. people under the control of a ruler or
    government

b. one chosen to head the government while a
    ruler is sick, absent, or very young

c. a farmworker, much like a slave, who
    belongs to the landowner

d. the title of any former emperor of Russia

e. skilled craftsperson

Abraham Lincoln and the Gettysburg Address

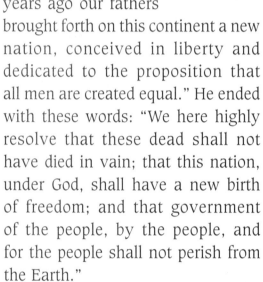

The United States of America was still less than 100 years old when it was torn in two by the Civil War. In 1861, bitter warfare broke out between the northern and southern states. The war was a clash of different ways of thinking, different customs, and different ways of life. In July of 1863, the tide of war turned in favor of the North. It was then that Union forces defeated Confederate troops at Gettysburg, Pennsylvania. During that three-day battle, the loss of life on both sides was staggering! More than 23,000 Union soldiers died. About 28,451 men were lost from the Confederate ranks.

On November 19 of the same year, ceremonies were held to dedicate a cemetery on the Gettysburg battlefield. President Abraham Lincoln was asked to say a few words. The president came prepared with a short speech written on the back of an envelope. Lincoln's "Gettysburg Address" would become one of history's most powerful calls for democracy, equality, and freedom.

Lincoln began his speech by saying, "Four score and seven years ago our fathers brought forth on this continent a new nation, conceived in liberty and dedicated to the proposition that all men are created equal." He ended with these words: "We here highly resolve that these dead shall not have died in vain; that this nation, under God, shall have a new birth of freedom; and that government of the people, by the people, and for the people shall not perish from the Earth."

The victory at Gettysburg and Lincoln's speech made a difference. His ringing declaration of democracy and equality seemed to promise that the end of the war was near. But the bitter battles and bloodshed continued until the Confederacy finally surrendered in 1865.

WORD SEARCH

1. What five-letter adjective from the reading means "of or within a country or government"? (Hint: It's part of the name of a major U.S. war.)

   c _____

2. What eleven-letter noun from the reading means "a public statement"?   _d_____

3. What eight-letter verb from the reading means "to open something or some place with a formal ceremony"?   _d_____

UNDERSTANDING THE SPEECH

Circle a letter to show how each sentence should be completed.

1. *Four score and seven* would be a period of

   a. 27 years.   b. 87 years.   c. 107 years.   d. 127 years.

2. When Lincoln refers to "our fathers," he means

   a. the Union generals.   c. Grandfather Lincoln.
   b. all American fathers   d. The founding fathers of
      and grandfathers.   the United States.

3. To "die in vain" means to:

   a. bleed to death.   c. die uselessly, for no good cause.
   b. die bravely.   d. die in a bloody battlefield.

4. A government "of the people, by the people, for the people" could best be described as a:

   a. dictatorship.   b. monarchy.   c. tyranny.   d. democracy.

ANALOGIES

Analogies are statements of relationship. To come up with the missing word, you must figure out the relationship between the first two words. Then complete each analogy with a word from the reading that shows the same relationship.

1. *North* is to *Union* as *South* is to _____.

2. *Dozen* is to *number 12* as *score* is to *number* _____.

3. *Reign* is to *rain* as *vein* is to _____.

4. *King* is to *monarchy* as *president* is to _____.

SYNONYMS

Complete the puzzle with words from the reading. Clue words are *synonyms* (words with a similar meaning) of the answer words.

ACROSS

4. proposal

6. graveyard

7. sour or harsh

DOWN

1. envisioned

2. to give up

3. land mass

5. die

COMPOUND WORDS

Unscramble the compound words to complete the sentences.

1. REFWRAA _____ raged for more than four years.

2. Many soldiers died on the FLEELABDITT _____.

3. The LOSBODHED _____ continued for four long years.

FIGURATIVE LANGUAGE

Figurative language is not intended to be taken literally. Read the sentence pairs below. In one sentence, the italicized word is an example of figurative language. In the other, the word or phrase has a literal meaning. Circle the letter of the sentence that contains figurative language.

1. a. The *tide* of war turned in favor of the North.

   b. The warship sailed on the outgoing *tide*.

2. a. The soldier was *staggering* from the blow to his head.

   b. The loss of life on both sides was *staggering*!

3. a. The United States of America was *torn in two* by the Civil War.

   b. The Union flag was *torn in two* by the Confederate soldiers.

Paul Revere's Ride

In April 1775, General Gage sent out British troops. Their mission was to destroy the American colonists' military supplies. The arms were stored at Concord, 20 miles from Boston. Throughout Massachusetts, patriot groups called *Minutemen* were ready to fight for freedom from Britain. Someone had to warn the Minutemen of Gage's attack!

This historical event inspired Henry Wadsworth Longfellow to write the now-famous poem, "Paul Revere's Ride." It begins:

Listen, my children, and you shall hear,
Of the midnight ride of Paul Revere.
On the eighteenth of April, in Seventy-Five;
Hardly a man is now alive
Who remembers that famous day and year.
He said to his friend, "If the British march
By land or sea from the town tonight,

Hang a lantern aloft in the belfry arch
Of the North Church tower, as a signal light.
One if by land and two if by sea;
And I on the opposite shore will be,
Ready to ride and spread the alarm
Through every Middlesex village and farm,
For the country folk to be up and to arm."

Seeing two lights in the steeple, Revere rode through the countryside and towns. As he rode, he warned colonists, "The British are coming!" Longfellow's poem concludes:

You know the rest. In the books you have read,
How the British regulars fired and fled—
So through the night rode Paul Revere;
And so through the night went his cry of alarm
How the farmers gave them ball for ball
From behind each fence and farm-yard wall,
Chasing the redcoats down the lane,
Then crossing the fields to emerge again
Under the trees at the turn of the road,
And only pausing to fire and load.

To every Middlesex village and farm,
A cry of defiance and not of fear,
A voice in the darkness, a knock at the door,
And a word that shall echo forevermore!
For, borne on the night-wind of the Past,
Through all our history to the last
In the hour of darkness and peril and need,
The people will waken and listen to hear
The hurrying hoof-beat of that steed,
And the midnight message of Paul Revere.

WORD SEARCH

1. What nine-letter plural noun from the reading means "people who settle in a distant land but are still under the rule of the country from which they came"?

   c_____

2. What six-letter noun from the reading means "a tower in which bells are hung"?

   b_____

3. What eight-letter plural noun is used to mean "members of an army that is maintained in peacetime as well as in war"?

   r_____

4. What six-letter verb means "to come out into view"?

   e_____

ANTONYMS

Complete the puzzle with words from the reading. Clue words are *antonyms* (words with the opposite meaning) of the answer words.

ACROSS

2. same

4. traitor

6. retreat

DOWN

1. obedience

3. safety

5. down low

COMPOUND WORDS

Answer each question below.

1. What compound word names colonial revolutionary groups?

   _____

2. What compound word did the colonists use as a name for British soldiers?

   _____

3. What compound word from the poem means "always"?

   _____

WORD FORMS

First, write the *adjective* form of each **boldface** noun from the reading. Check a dictionary if you need help.

1. **history** _____

2. **colonist** _____

3. **patriot** _____

4. **alarm** _____

VOWEL SOUNDS

Use a word from the reading to complete each sentence or phrase. (Hint: The words you need contain the vowels *ee* or *ea,* which have the long *e* sound.)

1. Two lights twinkled from the North Church _____.

2. Paul Revere mounted his _____ and rode through the night.

3. *One if by land and two if by* _____ . . .

4. *In the hour of darkness and peril and* _____ . . .

PARAPHRASING

To *paraphrase* means to put something you read into your own words. Paraphrase what you think Longfellow meant by the following lines.

1. *. . . For the country folk to be up and to arm.*

_____

_____

2. *. . . How the British regulars fired and fled . . .*

_____

_____

3. *The farmers gave them ball for ball.*

_____

_____

Vocabulary Stretch

Get out your dictionary and thesaurus! The challenging words in this lesson were especially chosen to stretch the limits of your vocabulary.

LOOK IT UP!

Complete each definition below with a word from the box. Check a dictionary if you need help.

aqueduct	autonomy	conspire	despot	dispatch
dominion	embark	isthmus	loyalist	meteorologist

1. _____ is a verb meaning "to plan together secretly."

2. An _____ is a channel or pipe for carrying water over a distance.

3. A cruel, unjust ruler who has complete control might be called a _____.

4. To begin or start out on a journey is to _____.

5. To maintain rule or power is to have _____.

6. To _____ is to send something out promptly to a certain place in order to do a certain job.

7. A _____ is a scientist who studies weather and climate.

8. Another word for self-government and independence is _____.

9. During a revolt, a _____ supports the present government.

10. An _____ is a narrow strip of land with water on both sides; it serves as a land bridge between two larger bodies of land.

WORDS IN CONTEXT

Use context clues to figure out which **boldface** word correctly completes each sentence. Circle the word.

1. The (**meteorologist / loyalist**) supported Britain's rule over the 13 colonies.

2. The emperor will (**dispatch / despot**) a messenger with news of the invaders' movements.

3. Many colonists wanted (**dominion / autonomy**) from England.

SYNONYMS

Complete the crossword puzzle with *synonyms* (words with a similar meaning) of the clue words.

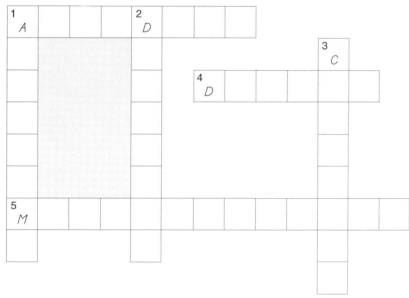

ACROSS

1. waterway, channel

4. tyrant, dictator

5. weather forecaster, climatologist

DOWN

1. independence, self-rule

2. control, supremacy

3. to scheme or plot

ANTONYMS AS CONTEXT CLUES

For each item, underline the word that appears in the box on page 24. Then find and circle a word that is its *antonym* (word with the opposite meaning).

1. George will embark on a dangerous mission. Hopefully, he will return with the information.

2. The king rewarded loyalists with favors and privileges. He punished traitors harshly.

3. The people overthrew the despot. They held a free election and chose a president.

4. We will dispatch the message at dawn. If the situation changes, we will send a second messenger to retrieve the document.

WORD CONNOTATIONS

Many words have a certain shade of meaning. They carry feelings and emotions that affect the way a reader feels. For example, the words *despot* and *ruler* are synonyms—but *despot* is a negative word, while *ruler* is neutral or even positive.

- Underline the word in each pair that has the most *positive* connotation.

    1. err / fail

    2. complain / whine

    3. bizarre / unusual

    4. evil / bad

    5. curious / nosy

    6. ambitious / industrious

    7. shifty / shrewd

    8. comedy / farce

    9. reckless / daring

    10. assistant / subordinate

    11. barren / infertile

    12. dry spell / drought

- Read the sentences below. Write a **plus (+)** if the italicized word has a *positive* connotation. Write a **minus (–)** if it has a *negative* connotation.

    1. _____ The king, who was a *confident* man, made up his own mind.

    2. _____ The *arrogant* king did not listen to his advisors.

    3. _____ Some called Samuel Adams a bold *rebel*.

    4. _____ Other people called Samuel Adams a *traitor* to England.

    5. _____ The soldiers made a *cautious* retreat.

    6. _____ The soldiers made a *cowardly* retreat.

REVIEW

Here's your chance to show what you've learned about the material you studied in this unit!

SENTENCE COMPLETION

To complete the sentences, write words from the readings in Unit 1.

1. Because they have the same meaning, the words *climate* and *weather* are called _s_____.

2. Although the words *ruler* and *tyrant* mean nearly the same thing, they carry different feelings, or _c_____.

3. Because they have opposite meanings, the words *conquer* and *surrender* are _a_____.

4. To _p_____ something is to rewrite it in your own words.

5. Words—such as *piece* and *peace*—that sound the same but have different meanings and spellings are _h_____.

6. _C_____ clues can help a reader figure out the meaning of an unfamiliar word.

COMPOUND WORDS

Write a *compound word* to answer the question or complete the sentence.

1. Farmers, shopkeepers, and craftspeople were ready to fight the British. Because they could come to arms at a moment's notice, these troops were known as _____.

2. Because their uniforms had scarlet-colored jackets, the British soldiers were known as _____.

3. What is a name for regions that are lower than the land around them? _____

4. Another way of saying that a place is across the ocean is to describe it as being _____.

5. What is a word for men of high social station who often gained their position by birth? _____

6. What do we call a piece of land where combat has taken place? _____

MYSTERY WORD PUZZLE

Unscramble the letters to write the word from the reading that matches each definition. Then write only the *circled* letters on the lines below. When you unscramble the letters, you will answer the question and spell the MYSTERY WORD.

1. Imaginary lines running east and west that measure distance in degrees: **TIDEGUNLO** __ __ __ __ __ __ __ __

2. One of the former rulers of the Russian empire: **RACZ** __ __ __ __

3. Places on Earth that are the farthest north and south: **LOSPE** __ __ __ __ __

4. Members of an army that is maintained in peacetime as well as in war: **SLAGRUER** __ __ __ __ __ __ __ __

5. All the recorded events of the past: **YISTHRO** __ __ __ __ __ __ __

Scrambled letters of mystery word (letters circled above): __ __ __ __ __ __ __ __ __

What do we call the study of the Earth and its features, including its climate, plants, animals, and minerals?

MYSTERY WORD: __ __ __ __ __ __ __ __ __

28

IN YOUR OWN WORDS

Paraphrase the following lines from President Lincoln's "Gettysburg Address."

Four score and seven years ago our fathers brought forth upon this continent a new nation, conceived in liberty and dedicated to the proposition that all men are created equal.

_____

_____

_____

_____

RECOGNIZING EXAMPLES

Write a letter to match each word in the first column with an example in the second column.

1. _____ **synonyms**   a. patriot, traitor

2. _____ **antonyms**   b. *serf* = from the Latin *servus,* meaning "slave"

3. _____ **compound word**   c. boundary, border

4. _____ **suffix**   d. colon*ist*

5. _____ **prefix**   e. battlefield

6. _____ **word origin**   f. *mid*night

MULTIPLE-MEANING WORDS

Each of the **boldface** words from Unit 1 has more than one meaning. Write two sentences for each word, using the word in two different ways.

1. **arms**

   SENTENCE **1:** _____

   SENTENCE **2:** _____

2. **coast**

   SENTENCE **1:** _____

   SENTENCE **2:** _____

PREVIEW

Test your knowledge of the vocabulary terms, skills, and concepts you will study in this unit. Answers are upside down on the bottom of the page.

TRUE OR FALSE?

Write **T** or **F** to show whether each statement is *true* or *false.*

1. _____ The words *federal* and *national* are synonyms.

2. _____ *Tropical* is the verb form of the noun *tropics.*

3. _____ The words *throne* and *thrown* are homonyms.

4. _____ A *jobless* person is one who has a very unimportant job.

5. _____ The words *allies* and *enemies* are antonyms.

6. _____ The phrase "passed away" is a euphemism for *died.*

7. _____ If you visited the *equator,* you would see a line in the Earth.

8. _____ The word *degree* has more than one meaning.

SPELLING

Circle the correctly spelled word in each group.

1. fertul / fertle / fertile

2. alliance / allyance / aliance

3. lattitude / latitude / latettude

4. infentry / infantry / enfantry

ANSWERS: TRUE OR FALSE? 1. T 2. F 3. T 4. F 5. T 6. T 7. F 8. T
SPELLING: 1. fertile 2. alliance 3. latitude 4. infantry

30

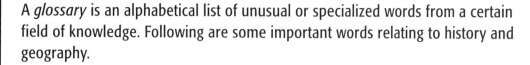

GLOSSARY

A *glossary* is an alphabetical list of unusual or specialized words from a certain field of knowledge. Following are some important words relating to history and geography.

alliance nations joined together, usually by a treaty, for certain purposes

city-state a city that governs itself as an independent political state

conquistador an early Spanish conqueror of Mexico and Peru

depression a period of time when business is very poor and many people lose their jobs

drought a long period of dry weather with little or no rain

equator an imaginary circle around the middle of the Earth; the equator is equally distant from the North and South Poles

federal having to do with the national government

globe a round model of the Earth showing the continents, oceans, and other important features

hero person admired for having done something brave or noble

infantry military troops trained and armed for fighting; "foot soldiers"

latitude distance north or south of the equator, measured in degrees

memorial anything, such as a statue or holiday, meant to honor and remind people of something or someone

plain a large stretch of flat land

treaty an agreement of cooperation among nations

tropics a mostly warm region of the Earth between the Tropic of Cancer and the Tropic of Capricorn (between about $23\frac{1}{2}°$ north and $23\frac{1}{2}°$ south)

valley low land lying among or between hills or mountains

veteran person who has served in the armed forces

volcanic containing molten rock, and having a likelihood of erupting

VOCABULARY IN CONTEXT

Complete each sentence with a word from the glossary. Use the other words in the sentence to help you decide which word to add. If you're still not sure, check the dictionary definition.

1. Cortez was a _____ who led the Spanish conquest of Mexico.

2. Blazing temperatures and a lack of rain led to the worst _____ in America's history.

3. The _____ of England, France, and the United States was a powerful force during World War II.

4. The _____ is a line of _____ that is measured at 0°.

5. Tall mountains ringed the lush, green _____ that lay below them.

MULTIPLE-MEANING WORDS

- Circle the word in each group that can have more than one meaning. Use a dictionary if you need help.

   1. infantry / city-state / plain   2. valley / depression / volcanic

- Now write two sentences for each word you circled. Give the word a different meaning in each sentence.

First Word: _____

   SENTENCE 1: _____

   SENTENCE 2: _____

Second Word: _____

   SENTENCE 1: _____

   SENTENCE 2: _____

SCRAMBLED WORDS

First unscramble the words from the reading. Then solve the crossword puzzle with the unscrambled words that complete the sentences.

MOLRIMAE _____   ROEH _____

DEEFRLA _____   REETNAV _____

CALCIVNO _____   LAPNI _____

LOGEB _____

ACROSS

1. The _____ mountain threatened to erupt and wipe out the village.

3. A stone wall was built as a _____ to those who fought in the Vietnam War.

6. The capital of the _____ government is in Washington, D.C.

DOWN

1. General Willis, who was a _____ of World War II, had some interesting tales to tell.

2. The large _____ of the world in the library shows the seven continents.

4. Because there were no hills, we could see for miles across the open _____.

5. Bruno the dog became a _____ when he saved his master's life.

EXAMPLES

Write the glossary word that is an example of each item.

1. word borrowed from Spanish:

2. homonym of *plane*:

3. antonym of *flood*:

_____   _____   _____

The Dust Bowl

The daytime sky was dark. Clouds of brown dust blotted out the sun. It had been extremely dry on the Great Plains. In fact, all of the early 1930s had been drier than usual in the Midwest. The midsummer heat—sometimes above 110°—baked the earth. Normally, waving grasses held the soil in place on the Great Plains. Without moisture, the grasses died and the parched ground cracked. When heavy winds came, the topsoil simply flew away. From 1933 to 1939, dust storms and drought turned good farmland into a desert of dust. Parts of Kansas, Colorado, New Mexico, Oklahoma, and Texas became known as the Dust Bowl.

The dust storms couldn't have hit Midwestern farmers at a worse time! America was facing an economic depression. Factories were closing, and people were out of work. Banks began to fail. Stocks became worthless. This was an era known as the Great Depression. When the farmers of the Great Plains lost their fields to wind and dust, they had no other way to earn a living.

The government offered the farmers what help it could. President Roosevelt sent millions of federal dollars to Dust Bowl states. The Soil Conservation Corps planted trees to hold the soil. But the rains didn't come. Winds continued to whip clouds of dust across the plains.

When the dust buried houses, fields, livestock, and wildlife, many farmers picked up and moved out. They hoped to find greener pastures in the West. But the western states were already filled with homeless, jobless Americans. Many of the Dust Bowl migrants ended up in California. There they crowded their families into wooden shacks. Families worked for a dollar a day picking fruits and vegetables in the fields. The Great Depression of the 1930s shattered the lives of many Americans. Among its worst victims were the farming families of the Dust Bowl.

WORD SEARCH

1. What seven-letter noun in the reading means "a long period of dry weather with little or no rain"?

    _d_ _____

2. What eight-letter plural noun in the reading
   names people who move from one place or
   country to another to make a new home?   *m*_____

SUFFIXES

- The suffix *-less* means "without." For example, a person who is "humorless" is
  without a sense of humor. Replace each **boldface** phrase below with a word from
  the reading that ends with the suffix *-less.*

  1. **without any value**

  2. **without employment**

  3. **without a place to live**

  _____   _____   _____

- Now write three sentences of your own. In each sentence, include a word that ends
  in the suffix *-less.*

  1. _____

  2. _____

  3. _____

IDIOMS

An *idiom* is an expression that has a meaning different from the literal meaning of the
words. For example, "to bury the hatchet" does not really mean to put the tool
underground. It is an idiom meaning "to forgive past quarrels; to make peace."
Circle a letter to show the meaning of each **boldface** idiom.

1. The Dust Bowl farmers hoped to find **greener pastures**
   in the West.

   a. a place where things are much better

   b. fields covered with green dollar bills

   c. grazing land for their cattle

2. When the stock market did poorly, everything else seemed
   to go to pot.

   a. became very moist

   b. got worse and fell apart

   c. got better, improved

WORD COMPLETION

Add vowels (*a, e, i, o, u*) to complete the words from the reading.
Use the context clues for help.

1. In order to stay alive, grasses and trees need m__ __st__r__.

2. President Roosevelt sent __c__n__m__c aid to the Dust Bowl.

3. The f__d__r__l government is headed by the U.S. president.

4. While the 1920s had been an __r__ of well-being, the 1930s brought tough times!

5. People sometimes invest money in st__cks, which means they buy shares in a business.

ANTONYMS

Complete the puzzle with words from the reading. Clue words are *antonyms* (words with the opposite meaning) of the answer words.

ACROSS

2. prosperity
4. mansions
5. succeed

DOWN

1. wastefulness
3. moist

COMPOUND WORDS

Compound words combine two or more words into one. Answer the questions containing **boldface** compound words from the reading.

1. Name three animals that are examples of **livestock**.

    _____   _____   _____

2. Where would you find **topsoil**? _____

    _____

3. What is the most likely use for **farmland**? _____

    _____

36

The World Wars

Students of history often find charts helpful—especially for comparing and contrasting. Charts can show you similarities and differences at a glance. The chart below compares and contrasts World War I and World War II.

	WORLD WAR I 1914–1918	**WORLD WAR II** 1939–1945
Causes	Growing power struggles erupt when Archduke Franz Ferdinand, heir to the throne of Austria-Hungary, is killed by a Serbian assassin.	Aggressive dictators become powerful: Hitler (Nazi party, Germany), Tojo (Japan); German invasion of Poland; Germany's Nazi campaign to kill all Jews
Alliances	Central Powers: Germany, Austria-Hungary Allies: England, France, Russia, Italy* (*Italy joined the Allies in 1915)	Axis nations: Germany, Japan, Italy Allies: England, France, Russia, United States, and many smaller nations
U.S. Involvement	United States declares war April 6, 1917	Japanese bomb Pearl Harbor; U.S. declares war on Dec. 11, 1941
New Technology	poison gas, fighter planes, tanks, trench warfare	submarines, atom bomb
Results	An Allied victory! A peace treaty drawn up in Versailles, and France sets up the League of Nations to promote world peace.	Allies are victorious! Victory in Europe (V-E Day) declared May 8, 1945. Japanese surrender on August 15, 1945; United Nations set up as peacekeeping organization

WORD SEARCH

1. What eight-letter noun in the reading means "nations or people joined together for some purpose, such as the uniting of nations by a treaty"?

   a _____

2. What eight-letter noun means "a ruler who has complete power"?

   d _____

3. What four-letter proper noun names a dictator-run political party that ruled Germany from 1933 to 1945?

   n _____

SYNONYMS

Complete the puzzle with words from the reading. Clue words are *synonyms* (words with a similar meaning) of the answer words.

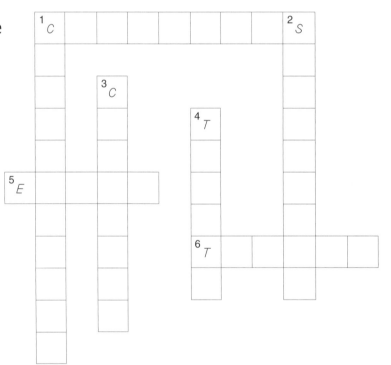

ACROSS

1. differences
5. to explode
6. a ditch

DOWN

1. similarities
2. U-boat (underwater boat)
3. crusade
4. agreement

HOMONYMS

Homonyms are words that sound the same but have different meanings and spellings. Circle the homonym that correctly completes each sentence. Then write an original sentence using the homonym you DID NOT circle. Use a dictionary for help.

1. Archduke Ferdinand was the (heir / air) to the kingdom of Austria-Hungary.

   _____

2. The Archduke was killed before he could sit on the (thrown / throne).

   _____

3. V-E Day celebrated (piece / peace) in Europe.

   _____

4. The United States developed the atom (bomb / balm) and used it to end the war with Japan.

   _____

5. (Plains / Planes) were first used for warfare during World War I.

   _____

ANALOGIES

Analogies are statements of relationship. To come up with the missing term, you must figure out the relationship between the first two terms. Then complete each analogy with a term from the reading that shows the same relationship.

1. *Poison gas* is to *World War I* as _____ _____ is to *World War II*.

2. *1914* is to *World War I* as _____ is to *World War II*.

3. *League of Nations* is to *World War I* as _____ _____ is to *World War II*.

4. *Mussolini* is to *Italy* as _____ is to *Germany*.

5. *Central Powers* are to *World War I* as _____ _____ are to *World War II*.

CONNOTATIONS

Connotations are the feelings and ideas associated with a word. Find the word *aggressive* in the reading. Then read the synonyms for *aggressive* listed below. Notice that some have positive connotations and others suggest negative feelings. Put a **+** or **–** beside each synonym to tell whether it is *positive* or *negative*.

1. _____ assertive   3. _____ combative   5. _____ determined

2. _____ bold   4. _____ militant   6. _____ pushy

Dogs of War

Long ago, "war dogs" joined hunting parties. They stood guard over campfires and accompanied Roman warriors into battle. Did you know that dogs have also served on modern battlefields? More than 1,000 canines trained by World War II marines became known as "Devil Dogs." Mainly Doberman pinschers, these dogs were used to sniff out mines, scout out enemy troops, and deliver supplies.

During the Vietnam War, civilians were asked to donate their dogs for duty. The U.S. Army and Marine Corps trained dogs—especially German shepherds—to use as sentries, or guards. The dogs were also enlisted for infantry duty. For this assignment they were taught to track, scout, and detect mines.

The war dogs of Vietnam served longer than most human soldiers. When a dog handler ended a tour of duty, the dog was reassigned to a new handler. Handlers of the 39th Infantry Scout Dog Platoon describe the loyalty of their canine companions. "He saved me many times, and others too," said Vietnam dog handler Carl Dobbins. He spoke emotionally of his wartime comrade, a German shepherd partner named Toro. For many Vietnam veterans, the names of famous war dogs like Toro, Buddha, and Baron are synonymous with the word *hero*.

Most of the canine heroes of the Vietnam War met a tragic end. Of the 4,000 or so dogs that served, fewer than 200 returned to the United States. Some were turned over to the South Vietnamese. Most were "put down"—a nicer way of saying they were killed.

Members of the Vietnam Dog Handlers Association have not forgotten their heroes. Through their efforts, a War Dog Memorial was erected at California's Riverside National Cemetery. The statue was dedicated in February 2000. Soon after, the president signed a bill protecting the dogs of war when they are no longer needed for service. This law requires the military to de-train the dogs and put them up for adoption by ex-military handlers.

WORD SEARCH

Answer the questions with words from the reading.

1. What eight-letter noun in the reading means "troops who are mainly trained to fight on foot"?

    i _____

2. What eight-letter noun in the reading means "the act of making one's own or taking into one's family"?

    a _____

3. What ten-letter adjective in the reading describes things that have the same meaning?

    s _____

4. What seven-letter noun in the reading means "a small group of soldiers, or a part of a company of soldiers"?

    p _____

5. What seven-letter noun names a person who has served in the armed forces?

    v _____

SYNONYMS

Complete the puzzle with words from the reading. Answer words are *synonyms* (words with a similar meaning) of the **boldface** words in each clue sentence.

ACROSS

2. A war dog usually had more than one dog **trainer**.

3. Dogs have been used to **find** mines and booby traps.

5. Most of the dogs of war met a **dreadful** end.

DOWN

1. Dogs were **drafted** to serve in the Vietnam War.

3. Americans were asked to **give** their dogs to the military.

4. In 2000, a war dog memorial was **built**.

PREFIXES

- Use your knowledge of *prefixes* to figure out the meanings of words from the reading. Draw lines to match each word in the first column with the correct definition in the second column.

1. **ex-military**   a. placed at some task or job another time

2. **de-train**   b. to cancel out previous teachings

3. **reassigned**   c. formerly in the armed services

- Now circle the word or words that best complete each sentence.

4. The prefix *ex-* means (in the past / again).

5. The prefix *de-* means (to undo or do in reverse / at an earlier time).

6. The prefix *re-* means (without / again).

MULPTIPLE-MEANING WORDS

Some words have more than one meaning, depending on how the word is used. Write two sentences for each **boldface** word below. In the first sentence, use the word as it was used in the reading. In the second sentence, use the word in an entirely different context with a different meaning. Use a dictionary for help.

1. **mines**

   SENTENCE 1: _____

   SENTENCE 2: _____

2. **parties**

   SENTENCE 1: _____

   SENTENCE 2: _____

3. **dedicated**

   SENTENCE 1: _____

   SENTENCE 2: _____

The Aztec Legend of *Tenochtitlan*

In central Mexico, volcanic mountains ring a large bowl of land. Around A.D. 1200, a group of wanderers arrived there to settle the region—the Valley of Mexico. Some of these people were a tribe who would become known as the Aztecs. Unfortunately, they drifted from the north just when wars between small city-states were being fought in central Mexico.

Forced to defend themselves, the Aztec nomads became excellent warriors. According to legend, they received word from Huitzilopochti (wheet-zee-loh-POHS-tlee)—their god of the sun and of warfare.

"Search for an eagle perched on a cactus!" the great god commanded. "The bird will grasp a snake in its beak. Where you find the eagle and cactus, build your city."

The legend says that the Aztecs finally saw the sign they were looking for. It was on a swampy island in Lake Texcoco (tay-SKOH-koh). There the tribe settled. They stopped hunting and became a farming society. They called their new home *Tenochtitlan* (tay-nawch-tee-TLAHN)—the "Place of the Cactus." In time, it became the heart of a great empire.

Because it was a swampland, Tenochtitlan could not grow enough crops to feed its population. So Aztec builders constructed reed rafts in shallow parts of the lake. They used tree branches to anchor these rafts to the lake bed. Then they blanketed the rafts with fertile mud from the lake bottom. The rich soil on these *chinampas*—or floating gardens—was ideal for growing corn, squash, and beans. This method of farming turned the swampy island of Tenochtitlan into a powerful capital city.

The Aztecs ruled there for hundreds of years—until the Spanish conquistadors arrived. In 1521, the Spaniards captured Tenochtitlan and conquered the Aztec empire. Today, Mexico City stands on the site where Tenochtitlan once stood.

WORD SEARCH

1. What eight-letter adjective in the reading describes a mountain that may erupt with molten rock that has built up inside?

   v _____

2. What six-letter noun in the reading means "low land that lies among or between hills or mountains"?

   v _____

3. What ten-letter plural noun in the reading means "cities that are independent political states, each with its own government"?

   c _____

4. What six-letter noun in the reading names a fleshy fruit that grows on a vine and can be cooked and eaten as a vegetable?

   s _____

WORDS AND MEANINGS

Writers often try to use verbs that create a colorful picture for the reader. Use the **boldface** verb in each sentence as a puzzle clue. The answer word will be a more colorful *synonym* (word with a similar meaning) from the reading.

ACROSS

1. The eagle will **hold** a snake in its beak.

4. The Spaniards **took over** Tenochtitlan.

5. The tribe **moved** down from the north.

DOWN

2. The eagle will be **standing** on a rock.

3. They **covered** the rafts with fertile soil.

BORROWED WORDS

Many words in English come from other languages. The word *conquistadors,* which appears in the reading, is borrowed from Spanish. So are the other words listed in the first column. Write a letter by the number to match each word with its meaning. Check a dictionary if you need help.

1. _____ **conquistadors**

2. _____ **mustang**

3. _____ **rodeo**

4. _____ **patio**

5. _____ **mesa**

6. _____ **bonanza**

7. _____ **adobe**

8. _____ **burro**

a. brick made of sun-dried clay

b. any of the early Spanish conquerors of Mexico and Peru

c. a very rich deposit of ore

d. a donkey

e. a small wild or partly wild horse of America's southwestern plains

f. a courtyard around which a house is built, or a paved area near the house

g. a large, high rock with steep sides and a flat top

h. competition in which contestants ride horses and rope cattle

PRONUNCIATION

Some of the difficult names in the reading are rewritten to help readers pronounce them correctly. The syllable (word part) written in capital letters is *accented* to show that it should be pronounced with the most emphasis. Example: Texcoco (tay-SKOH-koh)

Rewrite each **boldface** word from the reading to show how it is correctly pronounced. Divide each word into syllables. Write the accented syllable or syllables in capital letters. Use a dictionary if you need help. The first one has been done for you.

1. **Mexico**   _MEX i co_

2. **cactus**   _____

3. **legend**   _____

4. **Spanish**   _____

Special Lines of Latitude

Take a look at a globe of the world. Can you see lines that run east and west? These parallel lines, which are all the same distance from each other, are lines of latitude. They are imaginary lines used to measure distance between north and south.

Some lines of latitude have special names. The *equator*, for example, circles the center of the globe. Distances north and south of the equator are measured in degrees of latitude. They are numbered from zero to 90 in each direction. The 0° mark is on the equator. The 90° mark is on each pole.

The latitude line at 23½° north is called the *Tropic of Cancer*. The line at 23½° south is called the *Tropic of Capricor*n. The region between these two lines is known as the *tropics*. Most parts of the tropics have a very distinct climate. Year around temperatures there range from warm to hot. Only in the tropics does the sun ever shine directly overhead. These direct rays produce higher temperatures than slanted rays. In the tropics, the amount of daylight differs little from season to season. That means the temperature never changes very much.

Two more special lines of latitude are the *Arctic Circle* (66½° north) and the *Antarctic Circle* (66½° south). Some features of these regions are unlike anywhere else on the Earth. On the Arctic Circle's longest day of summer, about June 21, the sun never sets. During the shortest day of winter, about December 21, the sun never rises. The same phenomenon occurs in the Antarctic Circle at the opposite time of year. Just as winter comes to the Arctic Circle, summer begins in the Antarctic Circle.

GEOGRAPHY WORD SEARCH

1. What seven-letter noun in the reading means "an imaginary circle around the middle of the Earth that lies directly between the North and South Poles"?

    *e*_____

2. What eight-letter noun in the reading means "the distance north or south of the equator, measured in degrees"?   *l*_____

3. What five-letter noun in the reading means "a round model of the Earth showing the continents, oceans, and other important features"?   *g*_____

4. What eight-letter adjective in the reading describes things that are lying in the same direction, always the same distance apart, and never meeting?   *p*_____

SYNONYMS

Complete the puzzle with words from the reading. Clue words are *synonyms* (words with a similar meaning) of the answer words.

ACROSS

1. different
4. area
5. a happening
6. sloped

DOWN

2. unreal
3. contrary

WORD FORMS

Fill in the blank with a different form of the **boldface** word. Then use the word you wrote in an original sentence. The first one has been done for you.

1. **imagine** (verb) ___*imaginary*___ (adjective)
    The equator is an imaginary line that circles the globe.

2. **tropics** (noun) _____ (adjective)

_____

3. **differ** (verb) _____ (adjective)

_____

4. **distinct** (adjective) _____ (adverb)

_____

INFERENCE

Write a letter to match each **boldface** word on the left with its language source on the right. Check a dictionary if you need help.

1. _____ **arctic**

    a. from a Greek word meaning "the goat"; it is a sign of the zodiac that names a constellation of stars

2. _____ **antarctic**

    b. from the ancient Greek word *arktikos,* meaning "northern"

3. _____ **Capricorn**

    c. from the ancient Greek word *antarktikos,* which means "southern"

    d. from the Latin word *aequator,* which means "equalizer of day and night"

4. _____ **Cancer**

    e. from a Greek word meaning "the crab"; it is a sign of the zodiac that names a constellation of stars

5. _____ **equator**

THINKING ABOUT THE READING

Circle a letter to show how each sentence should be completed.

1. Only in the tropics is the sun ever

    a. cold.   b. directly overhead.   c. hidden for a whole day.

2. The Tropic of Cancer and the Tropic of Capricorn are

    a. lines of latitude that mark the edges of the tropics.

    b. star patterns seen in the night sky.

    c. other names for the North Pole and the South Pole.

Vocabulary Stretch

Get out your dictionary and thesaurus! The challenging words in this lesson were especially chosen to stretch the limits of your vocabulary.

WORDS IN CONTEXT

• Use a word from the box to complete each definition. Use a dictionary for help.

devastation	hostile	legislation	pacifist	recession

1. A _____ is a person who opposes war of any kind.

2. Although business is poor during a _____, economic times are not as bad as during a depression.

3. The dust storms of the 1930s brought _____ to the Great Plains of America's Midwest.

4. The U.S. Congress often enacts new _____ to protect the rights of citizens.

5. One who is _____ is unfriendly and may be warlike.

• Circle a word to correctly complete each sentence. Use context clues to help you select the appropriate word.

6. The (cartographer / legislation) drew a map that showed the new boundaries between counties.

7. Italy was a (devastation / fascist) state when it was ruled by the harsh dictator Mussolini.

8. In an act of (neutrality / genocide), Hitler ordered the murder of millions of Jews.

9. During World War II, Switzerland and Sweden both claimed (neutrality / recession) by refusing to take sides.

10. The Spaniards, who were newcomers to Mexico, conquered the Aztecs, who were an (indigenous / pacifist) tribe.

• Now write sentences of your own, using the **boldface** word choices you did *not* use to complete the sentences above.

11. WORD: _____   SENTENCE: _____

    _____

12. WORD: _____   SENTENCE: _____

    _____

13. WORD: _____   SENTENCE: _____

    _____

14. WORD: _____   SENTENCE: _____

    _____

15. WORD: _____   SENTENCE: _____

    _____

• Fill in the missing letters to complete words from the box on the previous page.

16. Otto became angry when the f__ __cis__ government of Nazi Germany practiced __en__ __id__ against Jews. Under such circumstances, Otto could not maintain n__u__ra__i__y. He was forced to take sides. Although Otto was a pa__i__ist and would not take up arms, he helped Jewish people escape the Nazis.

17. The Aztecs were one of the in__i__e__ __ __s tribes that first lived in Mexico. You might expect that the Aztecs would have been h__st__ __e toward the Spanish invaders. But on the contrary, the Aztecs believed the white men were gods, so they welcomed them with gifts. Their friendliness was a deadly mistake! It resulted in the de__as__at__ __n of the Aztec empire.

SYNONYMS

Complete the crossword puzzle with *synonyms* (words with a similar meaning) of the clue words.

ACROSS

5. law

DOWN

1. native

2. mapmaker

3. impartiality

4. destruction

ANTONYMS

Write a letter to match each **boldface** word with its *antonym* (word that means the opposite). If you need help, check a dictionary.

1. _____ **pacifist**   a. foreign

2. _____ **hostile**   b. friendly

3. _____ **recession**   c. warrior

4. _____ **fascism**   d. democracy

5. _____ **indigenous**   e. upturn

REVIEW

Here's your chance to show what you know about the material you studied in this unit!

ANALYZING WORDS

Complete each sentence with words from Unit 2. You have been given the first letter as a clue.

1. The *s*_____ -*less*, as in the word *homeless*, means "without."

2. The words *similarities* and *differences* are *a*_____.

3. The words *contrasts* and *differences* are *s*_____.

4. A *c*_____ is a person who makes maps.

5. *Swampland* and *wildlife* are examples of *c*_____ words.

6. A mountain that is likely to erupt can be described as *v*_____.

ANALOGIES

Remember that *analogies* are statements of relationship. Figure out the relationship between the first two words. Then complete each analogy with a word from Unit 2 that shows the same relationship.

1. *Brave* is to *fearful* as _____ is to *coward*.

2. *Longitude* is to *east-west* as _____ is to *north-south*.

3. *90°* is to the *North Pole* as *0°* is to the _____.

4. *Past* is to the prefix *ex-* as *again* is to the prefix _____.

HIDDEN WORDS PUZZLE

- Find and circle the words in the hidden words puzzle. Words may go up, down, across, backward, or diagonally. Check off each word as you find it.

___ **DEPRESSION**   ___ **SWAMPY**

___ **DROUGHT**   ___ **VICTORY**

___ **MIGRANT**   ___ **COMRADE**

___ **NOMAD**   ___ **TOPSOIL**

___ **CACTUS**   ___ **TROPICAL**

___ **TREATY**   ___ **VETERAN**

```
Y C T R E A T Y D S
D R O U G H T N E T
T S P M I L K A P N
R W S X R C B R R A
O A O D C A N E E R
P M I A A H D T S G
I P L M C G D E S I
C Y R O T C I V I M
A S W N U E Q F O H
L J U T S R P C N C
```

- Now use any six words from the puzzle in sentences of your own. Be sure that each sentence makes the word's meaning clear.

1. _____

2. _____

3. _____

4. _____

5. _____

6. _____

MAKE IT TRUE

Make each *false* statement *true* by replacing the **boldface** word. Write the replacement word on the line.

1. During the 1930s, a great **flood** caused much destruction on the Midwestern plains. _____

2. France and England were **enemies** during World War II.

   _____

3. Allies are usually **hostile** toward one another.

   _____

4. Some 4,000 **felines** served with the U.S. military forces in Vietnam.

   _____

5. *Conquistador* is a word borrowed from the **French** language.

   _____

6. The Tropic of Cancer marks the northern end of the **polar region**.

   _____

HOMONYMS

Write the *homonym* (word that sounds the same but has a different meaning and spelling) for each of the **boldface** words. Then use each homonym in a sentence. Make sure your sentence shows the meaning of the word.

1. **plain** / _____

   SENTENCE 1: _____

   SENTENCE 2: _____

2. **rain** / _____

   SENTENCE 1: _____

   SENTENCE 2: _____

3. **heir** / _____

   SENTENCE 1: _____

   SENTENCE 2: _____

4. **throne** / _____

   SENTENCE 1: _____

   SENTENCE 2: _____

PREVIEW

Test your knowledge of the vocabulary terms, skills, and concepts you will study in this unit. Answers are upside down on the bottom of the page.

TRUE OR FALSE?

Write **T** or **F** to show whether each statement is *true* or *false*.

1. _____ The words *symbol* and *emblem* are synonyms.

2. _____ The suffix *-ize* is often used to turn a noun into a verb.

3. _____ *Waterways, wildlife,* and *endanger* are all compound words.

4. _____ If an election is running "neck-and-neck," one candidate is far ahead.

5. _____ The Electoral College is a university in Washington, D.C.

6. _____ In the phrase "the rare white alligator," the word *rare* means "only slightly cooked."

7. _____ The abbreviation B.C. after a date means "before the birth of Jesus Christ."

8. _____ The abbreviation A.D. means "After Death" and refers to the time after the death of Jesus Christ.

SPELLING

Circle the correctly spelled word in each group.

1. campaign   campagne   campane

2. temple   tempel   tempul

3. pilosophy   philosophy   phillosofy

4. opress   oppres   oppress

GLOSSARY

A *glossary* is an alphabetical list of unusual or specialized words from a certain field of knowledge. Following are some important words that relate to history and geography.

bay a part of the sea that curves into the coastline

campaign a series of planned actions to accomplish something or get someone elected to office

candidate someone who runs for an office, position, or award

conservation the act of caring for and preserving forests, waters, and other natural resources

constitution a written document containing the basic rules of a government

election the process of choosing among candidates or issues by voting

Electoral College representatives of each state who meet to choose the president and vice president of the United States; these electors are expected to vote for the candidate who won in their own state

gulf a large part of the ocean—much bigger than a bay—reaching into the land

laws government rules telling people what they must and must not do

national park a large area of land maintained by the government for people to visit

oppress to control people by a cruel use of power

philosophy human thought about the meaning of life and about right and wrong behaviors

plague a deadly disease that spreads from person to person

politics the science of government

surrender to stop resisting and give up; to yield

swamp a piece of wet, spongy land

temple a building intended for worship of God or a god

WORDS IN CONTEXT

Complete each sentence with a glossary word. If you need help, check the dictionary definition.

1. The federal government sometimes sets aside a beautiful or historic area as a _____.

2. A deadly _____ killed nearly one-fourth of the city's population.

3. Her _____ of life was to treat others as she would like to be treated.

4. He used posters, newspaper ads, and speeches in his _____ for reelection.

5. Some recently passed _____ protect dogs from cruel treatment by their owners.

6. After half of his soldiers were killed, the general was forced to

_____.

MYSTERY WORD PUZZLE

Use the clues to figure out the glossary words that go across. Then complete the mystery word that reads from top to bottom.

ACROSS

1. a person who runs for office
2. the process of voting to select an officer or settle an issue
3. the science of government
4. a house of worship
5. the protection of valuable resources
6. to keep people down by treating them harshly

DOWN

THE MYSTERY WORD:
a government's written system of rules

1. C __ __ __ __ __ __ __ __ __

2. E __ __ __ __ __ __ __

3. P __ __ __ __ __ __ __

4. T __ __ __ __ __

5. C __ __ __ __ __ __ __ __ __ __

6. O __ __ __ __ __ __ __

WORD FORMS

Add *vowels* (*a, e, i, o, u*) to complete a different form of six glossary words. Use context clues for help.

1. A person who commits __nl__wf__l acts can be put in jail.

2. Citizens can help the environment by saving water and c__ns__rv__ng energy.

3. The code of rules told people what acts were illegal and what acts were l__wf__l.

4. Every four years Americans __l__ct a president.

5. After years of __ppr__ss__ __n, the citizens demanded their rights.

6. "What is the meaning of life?" is a ph__l__s__ph__c__l question.

ANALOGIES

Analogies are statements of relationship. Figure out the relationship between the first two words. Then complete each analogy with a word that shows the same relationship.

1. *Stream* is to *river* as *bay* is to _____.

2. *Telephone book* is to *phone numbers* as *constitution* is to _____.

3. *Dry* is to *wet* as *desert* is to _____.

4. *Research* is to *library* as *worship* is to _____.

MULTIPLE-MEANING WORDS

The glossary defines the words *gulf* and *bay* as they relate to geography. The same two words have different meanings in the sentences below. For help, use context clues or check a dictionary. Write a definition on the line after the sentence. (Use a dictionary if needed.)

1. The hound dogs often **bay** at the full moon.

   DEFINITION: _____

2. A **gulf** of misunderstanding separated the boy and the old man.

   DEFINITION: _____

The Florida Everglades

A one-hour drive from Miami takes travelers into the swamplands of the Everglades National Park. This area is like nowhere else in the world! The large region extends from Lake Okeechobee in the north to Florida Bay and the Gulf of Mexico.

Almost all of this spectacular wilderness is a shallow, slow-flowing river. It is home to many rare and endangered animals. There are alligators, pelicans, Florida panthers, and giant turtles weighing hundreds of pounds. In winter, the park draws many species of migrating birds from all over the country.

The northern Everglades is a prairie. It is covered by shallow water and saw grass—a grasslike plant with jagged edges which grows as high as 12 feet. The southern Everglades is a wilder, more remote region of salt marshes and swamps. Spreading roots of mangrove trees catch and hold soil there. Visitors are very likely to spot a rare green sea turtle or an American crocodile in the southern Everglades.

The town of Flamingo is the southernmost place in the continental United States. Once a sleepy fishing village, Flamingo now offers services for tourists including cottages and lodge rooms. Houseboats and canoes are available for cruising the waterways.

Peak tourist season is during the drier months between December and May. The temperature is cooler then, and a lower water level draws more wildlife. The wet season—from June to November—brings hotter weather, a decrease in migratory birds, and an increase in mosquitoes.

The Everglades are threatened by the rapid growth of surrounding cities. Chemicals pollute the water. Non-native plants can overpower native Everglades species. The state government and local conservation groups are working together to protect the Everglades. This unique swampland is truly a treasure worth saving.

WORD SEARCH

1. What nine-letter verb from the reading means birds moving from one place to another as the seasons change?   _m_____

2. What eleven-letter adjective from the reading describes something that has to do with one of the Earth's seven large land masses?

c _____

3. What twelve-letter noun from the reading means "the act of caring for and preserving forests, waters, and other natural resources"?

c _____

SYNONYMS

Complete the puzzle with words from the reading. Clue words are *synonyms* (words with a similar meaning) of the answer words.

ACROSS

2. a plain
4. sightseer
5. contaminate
6. one-of-a-kind

DOWN

1. sensational
3. swift
5. maximum

(crossword grid with numbered cells: 1 S, 2 P, 3 R, 4 T, D, 5 P, 6 U)

ANTONYMS

Complete each sentence with an *antonym* (word with the opposite meaning) of the **boldface** word.

1. Lake Okeechobee is at the **north** end of the Everglades, and the town of Flamingo is at the _____ end.

2. The temperature is **cooler** from December through May, and _____ from June to November.

3. The Everglades' waterways are not very **deep**, so canoes are used to cruise the _____ passages.

LATIN WORD ROOTS

In the selection, you read that the wet season brings an *increase* in mosquitoes. The word *increase* comes from the Latin root *cresco,* meaning "grow." What antonym of *increase* has the same root?

_____

PREFIXES

The prefix *en-* can mean "to put into or in" or "to make." *Endanger*, for example, means "to put in danger." Write a letter to match each word on the left with its meaning.

1. _____ **enliven**   a. to make weak

2. _____ **enrich**   b. to give hope and confidence

3. _____ **endear**   c. to make beloved

4. _____ **encrust**   d. to make more energetic

5. _____ **encourage**   e. to cover a layer

6. _____ **enfeeble**   f. to make richer

SUFFIXES

The suffix *-most* can be added to an adjective to form the superlative. For example, the *topmost* branch of a tree is the highest one. Answer the following questions about words that end with the suffix *-most*.

1. What word from the reading means "the farthest south"? _____

2. What word means "the farthest north"? _____

3. What word means "the first in position or importance"? _____

USING REFERENCE BOOKS

The reading mentions several animals that live in the Everglades. Choose one of these animals and look it up in a dictionary or encyclopedia. Then, describe the animal in two or three sentences.

ANIMAL: _____   DESCRIPTION: _____

_____

_____

_____

The Elephant and the Donkey

Readers are likely to discover political cartoons in their local newspapers—especially at election time. The drawings often picture a donkey and an elephant. As you may know, these animals represent the two main political parties of the United States. The donkey symbolizes the Democratic Party. The elephant is a Republican through and through! How in the world did these two unlikely characters become political symbols?

It was during the presidential election of 1828 that the donkey became associated with the Democrats. The Democratic candidate was Andrew Jackson. His opponents satirized his name, calling him a "jackass." Jackson laughed right along with his foes and adopted the donkey as his own emblem. He even used the symbol on his campaign posters. By the mid-1870s, the donkey had become the official political symbol of the Democratic Party.

One of the political cartoonists who popularized the Democratic donkey was Thomas Nast. Bavarian-born Nast moved to America at age six. In adulthood he became one of the country's most famous cartoonists. It was through Nast's imagination that the Republican elephant came onto the political scene. The elephant first showed up in a Nast cartoon in *Harper's Weekly* in 1874. In the sketch, an elephant labeled "the Republican vote" was being frightened by a donkey. Actually, the elephant had little to fear. Republican Ulysses S. Grant had defeated Democrat Horace Greeley and was serving a second term as U.S. president.

WORD SEARCH

1. What seven-letter noun from the reading means "a humorous drawing, sometimes meant to criticize or make fun of something"? c _____

2. What eight-letter noun from the reading means "the process of choosing by voting"? e _____

3. What nine-letter noun from the reading names someone who runs for office?

c _____

4. What four-letter noun from the reading means "the length that something lasts"?

t _____

ANTONYMS

Complete the puzzle with words from the reading. Clue words are *antonyms* (words with the opposite meaning) of the answer words.

ACROSS

2. foreign

3. unknown

4. teammate

DOWN

1. Republican

2. cried

3. hearten

ADJECTIVES

Unscramble the letters to write adjectives that match the meanings. (HINT: All the adjectives you write will end with the suffix *-ical*.)

1. Describes something having to do with politics: **LAPLOTCII** _____

2. Describes something that makes fun of or criticizes: **TILRISACA** _____

3. Describes wildly out-of-control fits of laughing or crying: **YESTALHRIC** _____

4. Describes something that is mysterious or spiritual: **MACLYTIS** _____

GREEK WORD ROOTS

The reading told about the symbol of the *Democratic* party. The Greek word root *demos* means "people." Draw a line to match each word based on the root *demos* with its meaning.

1. **democracy**

2. **demography**

3. **epidemic**

a. the rapid spread of a disease to many people

b. government in which the people hold ruling power

c. science that deals with factual information about groups of people

THINKING ABOUT THE READING

- Circle a letter to answer each question.

1. What quality might make a donkey a good political symbol?

   a. long ears   b. stubborn determination   c. loud hee-haw

2. What quality might make an elephant a good political symbol?

   a. a great memory   b. capacity for food   c. a long nose

- Write your ideas on the lines.

1. How did Andrew Jackson react when his opponents called him a name? Do you think this was a smart reaction? Why or why not?

   _____

   _____

   _____

   _____

2. If you were going to organize a political party, what animal might you use as a symbol? Why?

   _____

   _____

   _____

Neck-and-Neck Races to the White House

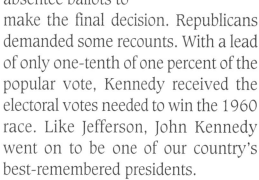

The outcome of the 2000 United States presidential election created national turmoil. Was the winner Democratic candidate Al Gore or Republican George W. Bush? The results were fiercely contested. The final decision: Bush had won Florida's electoral votes. That gave him the numbers he needed to become the U.S. president. But the new president faced a tough task. He had to convince citizens to unite and put post-election ill will aside. George W. Bush was not the first U.S. president to tackle such a job. Others have entered the White House under the shadow of a controversial victory.

Two of this country's most famous presidents, Thomas Jefferson and John F. Kennedy, won neck-and-neck races. In 1801, Jefferson and his opponent, incumbent John Adams, tied in the Electoral College. The final decision was left to the House of Representatives. It took 36 rounds of voting for representatives to elect Jefferson. It didn't take the new president long to get public support on his side. He went on to win a second term in a landslide election.

In the next century, Democrat John F. Kennedy won a very close race over Republican Richard Nixon. Some states depended on absentee ballots to make the final decision. Republicans demanded some recounts. With a lead of only one-tenth of one percent of the popular vote, Kennedy received the electoral votes needed to win the 1960 race. Like Jefferson, John Kennedy went on to be one of our country's best-remembered presidents.

Three more controversial races elected less-famous presidents. In 1825, none of the four candidates received an electoral majority. John Quincy Adams was declared president. In 1877, just one electoral vote pushed Rutherford B. Hayes over the number he needed for a victory. In 1888, Benjamin Harrison won the Electoral College—despite narrowly losing the popular vote!

Some 200 years ago, Thomas Jefferson sought to heal the wounds caused by a close election. He said, "Let us then, fellow citizens, unite with one heart and one mind. . . ." It is a fitting message for Americans of the 21st century.

WORD SEARCH

1. What nine-letter noun from the reading means "the person currently holding an office"?

   i _____

2. What six-letter noun from the reading means "a piece of paper on which a person casts a secret vote"?

   b _____

3. What eight-letter noun from the reading means "the greater part or number"?

   m _____

SYNONYMS

Complete the puzzle with words from the reading. Clue words are *synonyms* (words with a similar meaning) of the answer words.

ACROSS

2. debatable

5. of, for, or by the people

DOWN

1. triumph

3. uproar

4. job

PROPER NOUNS

- Draw a line to match each proper noun with its definition.

   1. **House of Representatives**   a. the official residence of the U.S. president and his family

   2. **Electoral College**   b. the lower branch of Congress; a federal lawmaking body

   3. **White House**   c. representatives from each state who vote to elect the president and vice president

• Now select one of the three proper nouns. Use an encyclopedia or history book to find out another fact about the item you chose. Write the fact on the lines below.

_____

_____

LATIN WORD ROOTS

The words in the first column are built on the root Latin *centum*, which means "hundred." Write a letter to match each word with its meaning.

1. _____ **century**
2. _____ **cent**
3. _____ **percent**
4. _____ **centigrade**
5. _____ **centimeter**
6. _____ **centurion**

a. officer in the Roman army commanding a company of 100 foot soldiers

b. period of 100 years

c. unit of length equal to 1/100th of one meter

d. describing a thermometer on which freezing is 0° and boiling is 100°

e. coin worth 1/100th of a dollar

f. a hundredth part; the symbol is %

IDIOMS

Idioms are figurative rather than literal expressions. A "neck-and-neck" race, for example, is very close right up to the finish line. The phrase refers to horses racing side by side until one stretches its neck out to cross the finish line first. Circle a letter to show the meaning of each italicized idiom.

1. Thomas Jefferson won a second term of office in a *landslide election*.

   a. few voters because of heavy rain
   b. an overwhelming victory
   c. the day of an earthquake

2. Two hundred years ago, Thomas Jefferson sought to *heal the wounds* caused by a close election.

   a. get past hard feelings
   b. treat those injured in war
   c. conduct a recount of votes

The Code of Hammurabi

If a man breaks into a house, he shall be killed in front of that house and buried there.

That is just one law in Hammurabi's Code. Hammurabi (hah moo RAH bee) was among the greatest kings of the ancient Middle East. He ruled the great kingdom of Babylonia from about 1792 B.C. to 1750 B.C.

Hammurabi sought to unite his empire by publishing a set of laws. Many of the rulings had been around for a long time. But Hammurabi wanted to make it clear that his subjects must follow them. He ordered artisans to carve nearly 300 laws on a pillar. The seven-foot stone column stood in the capital city of Babylon. Hammurabi's Code became history's first major collection of laws.

At the top of the pillar, a carving showed Hammurabi sitting on his throne. These engraved words declared the king's goal: *That the strong may not oppress the weak.*

The Code of Hammurabi dealt with many aspects of life. There were laws about marriage and divorce, property, business contracts, wages, loans, and military service. The Code spelled out lawbreakers' penalties. By the standards of A.D. 2000, some of these punishments seem harsh. Hammurabi believed in the principle of "an eye for an eye; a life for a life." Imagine, for example, that a house collapsed due to poor construction. If someone in that house was killed, the builder could be put to death. This was Hammurabi's idea of justice!

While its punishments were harsh, Hammurabi's Code showed a concern for human rights and welfare. Borrowers, for example, did not have to repay their loans if personal misfortune made it impossible to do so. The code also allowed a wife to own property and leave it to her children.

Eventually, invaders conquered the Babylonians. Hammurabi's laws, however, were passed down through the ages. Many of his ideas are reflected in today's laws.

WORD SEARCH

1. What two-letter abbreviation stands for the words "Before Christ"? (used to date events before the year Jesus Christ was born)

   _____

2. What two-letter abbreviation stands for the Latin words "Anno Domini"? (used to date events from the year Jesus Christ was born)

   _____

WORD MEANINGS

Unscramble the word in each clue. Then complete the puzzle with the unscrambled words.

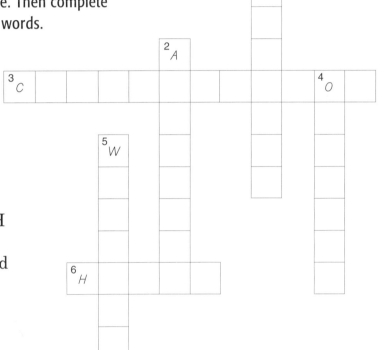

ACROSS

3. The noun SOICNOTCUTNR means something that has been built; a structure.

6. The adjective HRASH describes something that is unusually hard or cruel.

DOWN

1. The noun TECIJSU means the quality of being fair and lawful.

2. The plural noun SITSNAAR means craftspeople who are skilled in some trade.

4. The verb REPPSSO means to keep people under control by a cruel use of power.

5. The noun LEFREAW means the health, happiness, and general well-being of a people.

POSSESSIVES

Possessives are words that show ownership. Singular nouns are made possessive by adding an apostrophe (') and an *s* (*Mary's* sweater). Plural nouns that end in *s* are made possessive by adding an apostrophe after the *s* (five *countries'* flags). Plural nouns that do *not* end in *s* are made possessive by adding an apostrophe and an *s* (the *children's* rooms).

- Circle the possessive noun in each sentence.

    1. Hammurabi's Code was engraved on a stone pillar.

    2. This was history's first published set of laws.

    3. Lawbreakers' punishment could be harsh.

- Read each sentence below. Write the possessive form of the noun in parentheses. The first one has been done for you.

    4. Hammurabi was thinking of his (people) welfare.   _____*people's*_____

    5. The (Babylonians) kingdom was governed by strict laws.   _____

    6. The (kingdom) ruler was Hammurabi.   _____

PREFIXES AND SUFFIXES

Underline the *prefix* (word part added to the beginning) or *suffix* (word part added to the end) in each word. Next, write the meaning of the word part you underlined. (Check a dictionary if you need help.) Finally, write another word that has that same prefix or suffix.

1. **misfortune**   WORD PART MEANING: _____

    ANOTHER WORD: _____

2. **powerless**   WORD PART MEANING: _____

    ANOTHER WORD: _____

3. **greatest**   WORD PART MEANING: _____

    ANOTHER WORD: _____

Athens and Sparta

The ancient Greek empire was a mountainous land. It included many small islands that were separated by seas. Because of this geography, contact between regions was difficult. The empire's city-states maintained individual governments and built their own power.

Each city-state had its unique idea about the way people should live. Some were ruled by a single leader. Others gave citizens a voice in government. Sometimes the city-states supported each other as allies. At other times, they challenged each other's power. In the two largest city-states—Athens and Sparta—citizens led very different lives!

Sparta was a military society governed by a small group of men. A Spartan boy was raised to be a soldier. A Spartan girl was thought to be useless as a warrior—and thus without value. Most of the work in Sparta was done by slaves. The Spartan men were usually off fighting in the army. The Spartans had little interest in philosophy, art, or music.

By contrast, the Athenians gave less thought to warfare. Athens was a wealthy city. Its wealth allowed the people to enjoy life. They created marble statues, built fine temples, and made their city one of the most beautiful in the world. Actors performed plays in outdoor amphitheaters. Great teachers, like Socrates, encouraged Athenians to question their world and think about right and wrong. Athenians developed a democratic government. A constitution declared that all free men were citizens with the right to vote. While Athenians did have slaves, some citizens questioned the practice. Many other Greek city-states admired the Athenian way of life and adopted their ideas of democracy.

Sparta, however, greatly resented Athens' growing power. In 421 B.C., Sparta led some other city-states in a war for control of Greece. This war, called the Peloponnesian War, lasted 27 years! It finally ended when a plague broke out in Athens. With one-fourth of its population dead from the illness, Athens could no longer hold out. In 404 B.C. Athens finally surrendered to Sparta.

WORD SEARCH

1. What seven-letter plural noun from the reading means "land masses smaller than continents and surrounded by water"?   _i_ _____

2. What ten-letter noun from the reading means "the study of human thought about the meaning of life and about right and wrong"?   _p_ _____

3. What ten-letter noun from the reading means "all the people living in a country, city, or other specific region"?   _p_ _____

WORD MEANINGS

Use the clues to complete the puzzle with words from the reading.

ACROSS

3. captive servants
5. house of worship
7. felt angry about

DOWN

1. a body of laws
2. quarreled about
3. backed up
4. sculpted likenesses
6. because of this

UNDERSTANDING THE ABBREVIATIONS

Earlier in this unit, you learned that historical dates may be labeled B.C. or A.D. Numbers followed by B.C. are dated from before the birth of Jesus Christ. Numbers preceded by A.D. are dated from after the birth of Christ. According to the reading, the Peloponnesian War began in 431 B.C. and ended in 404 B.C. Use this information to answer the following questions.

1. Which came first, 431 B.C. or 404 B.C.?   _____

2. Which came first, 2000 B.C. or 31 B.C.? _____

3. Which came first, A.D. 1994 or 2404 B.C.? _____

4. Which came first, A.D. 1999 or A.D. 1521? _____

5. From 550 B.C. to 479 B.C. the Persians tried to conquer Greece. Their many attacks failed. Which came first, the Peloponnesian War or the Persian Wars? _____

6. When using the abbreviation B.C., which comes first—the date or the abbreviation? _____

7. When using the abbreviation A.D., which comes first—the date or the abbreviation? _____

THINKING ABOUT THE READING

Think about the similarities and differences between Sparta and Athens. Then complete the *Venn diagram* below. In the first section, list qualities unique to Sparta. In the last section, list qualities unique to Athens. In the center section, list qualities shared by both Athens and Sparta.

SPARTA	BOTH	ATHENS
_____	_____	_____
_____	_____	_____
_____	_____	_____
_____	_____	_____

USING THE DICTIONARY

The word *Spartan* is still part of our language today. Look up *Spartan* in a dictionary and write the meaning below.

_____

_____

Vocabulary Stretch

Get out your dictionary and thesaurus! The challenging activities in this lesson were designed to stretch the limits of your vocabulary.

COMPLETION

Complete each definition with a word from the box. Use a dictionary for help.

| administration | Congress | ecology | siege | harbor |
| unconstitutional | propaganda | isolated | foliage | elector |

1. An _____ is a member of the Electoral College or any person who has the right to vote in an election.

2. _____ is the group of elected officials in the U.S. government that makes laws; it has two parts: the Senate and the House of Representatives.

3. Something that is not allowed by the government or does not conform to the written laws can be called _____.

4. _____ consists of often false or misleading ideas that are spread to do damage to the opposition.

5. The _____ includes the president and those working with him in the federal government.

6. Ships and boats may safely anchor in a _____.

7. _____ is the study of the relationship between living things and the conditions that surround and affect them.

8. Something that is _____ is alone, secluded, or set apart.

9. A _____ occurs when an army tries to capture a city or fort by surrounding it for a long period of time.

10. The leaves of trees or plants are called their _____.

USING CONTEXT CLUES

Use *context clues* to figure out which word correctly completes each sentence.
Circle the word.

1. The Spartan warriors laid (foliage / siege) to the city-state of Athens.

2. The (administration / elector) cast her one vote for candidate Mario Mendelson.

3. Some voters did not like Mario, who had spread some exaggerated (propaganda / ecology) about his opponent.

RECOGNIZING EXAMPLES

Look at the boxed words on the previous page. Then tell which word . . .

1. . . . has a prefix that means "not"?   _____

2. . . . is a proper noun?   _____

3. . . . has a suffix that means "one who does something"?   _____

4. . . . uses the suffix *-ion* to make a verb into a noun?   _____

5. . . . follows the spelling rule "*i* before *e* except after *c*"?   _____

SUFFIXES

The suffix *-al* is often used to build adjectives. Circle the correctly spelled adjective in each group. (Use a dictionary if you need help.) Then use the correctly spelled adjective in a sentence.

1. congressional   congresionel   congressial   congressal

   SENTENCE: _____

2. ecologial   ecologal   ecological   eclogical

   SENTENCE: _____

3. electral   electoral   electrocal   electional

   SENTENCE: _____

75

MATCHING

Match each item on the left with the word that describes it. Write a letter by each number.

1. _____ George W. Bush and his cabinet   **a. isolated**

2. _____ "I refuse to hire women!"

3. _____ "I want everyone to know that   **b. propaganda**
candidate Mario Mendelson once
flunked high school algebra!"

                                                 c. administration

4. _____ The team of scientists will live
alone at a remote Antarctic post.

                                                 d. ecology

5. _____ Old-growth forests should be
maintained to protect certain
birds and animals.   **e. unconstitutional**

COMBINING WORD PARTS

• The word part *-ology* means "the science or study of." What word from the box on page 74 has the word part *-ology,* and what does it mean?

WORD: _____   MEANING: _____

_____

• Now complete each sentence with one of the following words. Use a dictionary for help.

anthropology	psychology	archeology	geology

1. The study of the Earth's crust, rocks, and fossils is called

   _____.

2. _____ is the study of the human mind and the

   reasons behind people's actions.

3. The science that studies the origin, development, and customs of

   human beings is called _____.

4. The science of _____ studies ancient times and

   ancient life by examining ruins, artifacts, and tombs.

UNIT 3

REVIEW

Here's your chance to show what you know about the material you studied in this unit!

SENTENCE COMPLETION

Write words from Unit 3 to complete each sentence.

1. Both _b_____ and _g_____ are parts of the sea that curve into the land.

2. _C_____ is the act of caring for and protecting the land.

3. The United States has many _n_____ _p_____, which are lands set aside and preserved by the federal government.

4. A person seeking another term of office is an _i_____.

5. A _c_____ is a government's written code of laws.

SHOW YOUR UNDERSTANDING

Circle the letter of the correct answer.

1. What would you be most likely to do in an *amphitheater*?

   a. see a performance   b. purchase a souvenir

2. What happens during a *campaign*?

   a. tourists take a canoe trip   b. candidates try to attract voters

3. Which words best describe the *donkey* and the *elephant*?

   a. political candidates   b. political symbols

4. Someone described as *Spartan* would have which traits?

   a. concerned with ecology and involved in conservation   b. brave, disciplined, and strict

HIDDEN WORDS PUZZLE

- Find and circle the words in the puzzle. Words may go up, down, across, backward, or diagonally.

___ SWAMP	___ MIGRATE
___ SURRENDER	___ CARTOON
___ MAJORITY	___ ECOLOGY
___ BALLOT	___ PLAGUE
___ ISLAND	___ CANDIDATE
___ ELECTION	___ TEMPLE
___ POPULATION	

```
B  C  A  N  D  I  D  A  T  E
J  A  M  K  E  N  A  E  O  P
R  B  A  L  L  O  T  L  Y  O
S  T  J  V  I  X  E  E  G  P
W  U  O  M  O  I  M  C  O  U
A  N  R  E  U  S  P  T  L  L
M  B  I  R  T  L  L  I  O  A
P  E  T  M  E  A  E  O  C  T
K  F  Y  O  R  N  R  N  E  I
U  S  V  M  A  D  D  G  L  O
C  A  R  T  O  O  N  E  I  N
P  L  A  G  U  E  W  H  R  M
```

- Now use each word in a sentence of your own. Be sure that your sentence makes the word's meaning clear.

1. _____

2. _____

3. _____

4. _____

5. _____

6. _____

7. _____

8. _____

9. _____

10. _____

11. _____

12. _____

13. _____

EXAMPLES

Match items on the left with words on the right. Write a letter by each number.

1. _____ antonyms

2. _____ synonyms

3. _____ possessives

4. _____ compound words

5. _____ Greek root that means "the people"

6. _____ Greek word part that means "on all sides" or "around"

a. *conserve* and *waste*

b. *demos* as used in *democracy*

c. king's code, people's laws, voters' ballots

d. *amphi-* as used in *amphitheater*

e. outdoor, wildlife, city-states

f. *artisan* and *craftsperson*

PREFIXES AND SUFFIXES

To complete each sentence, add a *prefix* or *suffix* from the box to the *italicized* word. The new word should have the same meaning as the phrase in parentheses.

> **PREFIXES:** *en-*   *re-*   *mis-*   **SUFFIXES:** *-less*   *-ers*   *-ee*

1. When a plague swept Athens, the people were (without *power*) _____ against the warriors of Sparta.

2. The (people who *invade*) _____ were mighty warriors.

3. The growth of cities near the Everglades has (put into *danger*) _____ the waterways and the wildlife.

4. When an election result is in question, officials may (*count* again) _____ the ballots.

5. The candidate had the (bad *fortune*) _____ of becoming ill during the election campaign.

6. Ballots from (those who were *absent*) _____ voters will be counted next week.

UNIT 4

HISTORY AND GEOGRAPHY WORDS

PREVIEW

Test your knowledge of the vocabulary terms, skills, and concepts you will study in this unit. Answers are upside down on the bottom of the page.

TRUE OR FALSE?

Write **T** or **F** to show whether each statement is *true* or *false*.

1. _____ A *pharaoh* and a *chief* are both leaders.

2. _____ The words *retreat* and *advance* are synonyms.

3. _____ The color *golden* sometimes symbolizes wealth.

4. _____ An *archeologist* is a scientist who forecasts the weather.

5. _____ You'd be likely to find a *monsoon* in a buried tomb.

6. _____ The words *afterlife* and *lifelike* are compound words.

7. _____ A *legend* is a story that has been proven scientifically true.

8. _____ *Seasonal* is the adjective form of the noun *season*.

SPELLING

Circle the correctly spelled word in each group.

1. pharoah   pharaoh   faroh

2. immigrants   imigrents   immagrunts

3. fronteer   fronteir   frontier

4. debris   debri   dabris

ANSWERS: True or False? 1. T 2. F 3. T 4. F 5. F 6. T 7. F 8. T
Spelling: 1. pharaoh 2. immigrants 3. frontier 4. debris

80

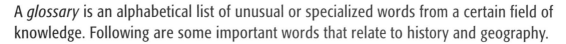

GLOSSARY

A *glossary* is an alphabetical list of unusual or specialized words from a certain field of knowledge. Following are some important words that relate to history and geography.

archeologist a scientist who studies ancient times and peoples by digging up the remains of past civilizations

autobiography the story of a person's life, written by that person

chief the leader or head of a group

cowboy a ranch worker who rides horses and tends cattle

economy a system of producing and using wealth

frontier the part of a settled country that borders the wilderness

graph a chart that uses lines and bars to show the changes taking place in something

immigrants people who come into a foreign country in order to make a new home

legend a story, probably untrue, that has been handed down through the years

monsoon a seasonal wind caused by temperature differences between land and sea

mummy a body, often wrapped in cloth strips, kept from decaying by the use of chemicals

museum a building or room for preserving and displaying things that are important to history, art, or science

pharaoh the title of the rulers of ancient Egypt

reservation public land set aside for some special use; the U.S. government, for example, moved Native Americans to such lands

retreat a withdrawal or turning back from danger

rodeo a competition that usually includes horseback riding, cattle roping, and other cowboy skills

tribe a group of people living together under the guidance of a leader

WORDS IN CONTEXT

Complete each sentence with a word from the glossary. Check the dictionary or use context clues (other words in the sentence) if you need help.

1. The _____ unearthed some ancient bowls
   carved from wood.

2. In his _____, the governor writes about his childhood in Kansas.

3. On a field trip to the _____, students saw Native American pottery and masks.

4. "First up in this _____ event," the announcer said, "is Bronco Bob from the Lazy R Ranch."

5. The _____ tried to calm his angry young warriors and avoid a war.

6. The tribe was forced from its native lands and onto a

_____.

WORD HISTORY

Some glossary words have origins in other languages. Write a letter to match each word on the left with its origin. Use a dictionary if needed.

1. _____ **rodeo**   a. from an Arabic word meaning "time" or "season"

2. _____ **pharaoh**   b. containing the Greek word part *archaeo-* which means "ancient" or "primitive"

3. _____ **monsoon**
                         c. from an Egyptian word meaning "great house"

4. _____ **museum**
                         d. from a Spanish word meaning "cattle ring"

5. _____ **archeologist** e. from a Greek word meaning "place of study"

WORD FORMS

Add vowels (a, e, i, o, u) to complete a different form of a word from the glossary. Use context clues for help.

1. Ellis Island was an __mm__gr__t____n center in New York harbor.

2. The book was an ____t__b____gr__ph__c__l account of the life of an American cowboy.

3. The science of __rch__ __l__gy studies past times and ancient people by examining ancient ruins.

4. It is a tr__b__l custom for boys to go on their first hunt at age 13.

5. Deep within the tomb, the explorers uncovered the m__mm__f__ __d body of the king.

SCRAMBLED WORDS

First unscramble the words from the glossary. Then solve the crossword puzzle with words that complete each sentence.

WOYCOB _____   RIBET _____

RATSMIMGNI _____   NIFROTRE _____

YUMMM _____   NOMOSON _____

ACROSS

2. When it blew in from the sea, the summer _____ brought heavy rains.

4. The well-wrapped _____ had been preserved in its tomb for thousands of years.

6. The pioneers moved west to settle the new _____.

DOWN

1. Every _____ needs a horse, a saddle, and a rope.

3. Many ____ from Russia and Eastern Europe settled on the west coast of the United States.

5. Sitting Bull was the powerful leader of a Native American _____.

Nat Love: From Slave to Cowboy

Nat Love was born in Tennessee in June of 1854. Like most slaves, he never knew his exact birthday. Nat and his family belonged to a man named Robert Love. When the Civil War freed the slaves, Nat's family took Mr. Love's name as their own.

Nat's father died when he was 14. Nat worked at odd jobs to help support the family. It quickly became clear that the boy had a way with animals. Word spread that for 10 cents Nat Love could break any horse!

In 1869, Nat moved out west. That was the place for a bronco buster to get good jobs! Promising to send money home, he hitched rides on farmers' wagons, hopped freight trains, and walked westward. Nat was heading for Dodge City, Kansas—a real cowboy town!

Nat got jobs on one ranch after another. Each rancher was awed by his horsemanship. On July 4, 1876, he found himself in Deadwood, South Dakota. Independence Day celebrations there included a rodeo. Nat set a record for riding, roping, and shooting. He won $200 in prize money and earned a new nickname. From that day forward, his alias was Deadwood Dick.

When railroad lines stretched into the West, Nat knew that times were changing. In 1890, he got a job as a porter on one of the fancy new train cars called Pullmans. Now he rode the plains on a train instead of a horse.

In 1907, Nat wrote his life story. It was titled *The Life and Adventures of Nat Love, Better Known in the Cattle Country as Deadwood Dick*. The autobiography was full of tales about Nat's own adventures. He also told about western characters such as Billy the Kid, Buffalo Bill, and Jesse James. Nat described how he shot the Colt .45's out of the hands of five gunmen. And he told how a Native American tribe made him their "black brother." Nat Love left his mark on the frontier and became one of the most famous names in the West.

WORD SEARCH

1. What six-letter noun names a ranch worker who rides horseback and tends horses and herds cattle?

    c_____

2. What eight-letter noun from the reading means "the part of a settled country that borders the wilderness"? _f_____

3. What seven-letter adjective from the reading describes the type of train that carries cargo? _f_____

4. What six-letter noun from the reading means "a person who carries luggage or who assists passengers on a train"? _p_____

SYNONYMS

Complete the puzzle with words from the reading. Clue words are *synonyms* (words with a similar meaning) of the answer words.

ACROSS

2. attendant

4. festivities

5. amazed

DOWN

1. tales

3. relocated

WORD PARTS

Use information from the reading to answer the following questions.

1. What word from the reading adds **two** word parts to the root word *horse*? _____

2. What two word parts are added to make the new word? _____ and _____

3. What is the meaning of the new word? (Use a dictionary if you need help.)

_____

4. What word contains the same two word parts and means "the ability or skill needed to put on an interesting, exciting *show*"? _____

5. What word contains the same word parts and means "skill as a *worker*" or "the skill of a worker in doing some craft"? _____

MULTIPLE-MEANING WORDS

A word can have different meanings in different contexts. Circle the meaning of the **boldface** word as it is used in the reading.

1. to **break** a horse

   a. to split apart by force   b. to tame by using force

2. **hitched** rides

   a. traveled by catching rides   b. moved upward with a quick jerk

3. work at **odd** jobs

   a. strange or bizarre   b. occasional, not regular

IDIOMS

The words in an *idiom* are not meant to be understood literally. For example, "to eat humble pie" does not really mean to swallow a pastry. This expression means to humble yourself by admitting to a mistake. Circle a letter to show each idiom's meaning.

1. Nat Love *left his mark* on the West.

   a. drew lines in the dust   b. had a noticeable effect on

2. When Nat headed west, some folks said he should not *chase a rainbow*.

   a. have big dreams and unrealistic expectations

   b. leave home during the rainy season

3. Nat's rodeo victory in Deadwood was *a feather in his cap*.

   a. an especially glorious achievement   b. cowboy hat decoration

Ellis Island: The Golden Door

Ellis Island was the port of entry for more than 16 million immigrants to the United States. Some called this island in New York Harbor the "Gateway to the New World." Others saw it as a "Golden Door" to opportunity. For yet others, it was a scary place—an "island of tears." Newcomers, most of whom did not speak English, had to answer questions. "Do you have relatives in America? Have you got a job? Have you ever been arrested?" Doctors checked each person's physical and mental health. Actually, few newcomers were sent home.

About 98 percent of those examined at Ellis Island were allowed to enter the country.

The U.S. government used Ellis Island as an immigration station from 1892 until 1924. The station closed completely in 1954. In 1965, the island became a national historic site, part of the Statue of Liberty Monument.

The graph below shows the flow of new arrivals during America's peak years of immigration. Remember that Ellis Island served as the main port of entry from 1892 until 1924.

AMERICA'S NEWCOMERS, 1820–1929

Number of Immigrants (in millions)

Years	1820–1829	1830–1839	1840–1849	1850–1859	1860–1869	1870–1879	1880–1889	1890–1900	1900–1909	1910–1919	1920–1929

WORD SEARCH

1. What ten-letter plural noun from the reading means "those who come into a foreign country to make a new home"?

    *i*_____

2. What eight-letter noun from the reading means "something, such as a statue or building, erected in memory of people or events"?

    *m*_____

3. What eight-letter noun from the reading means "official identification a person uses when traveling in foreign countries"?

    *p*_____

COLORS AS SYMBOLS

The reading explains that many immigrants saw Ellis Island as a *Golden Door*. Gold is often used to stand for, or *symbolize,* good things—wealth, good times, good fortune. Many colors stand for ideas or feelings. Use context clues to figure out which idea the **boldface** color symbolizes in each sentence below. Circle the letter of your choice.

1. The **red** warning sign was posted next to the elevator.

    a. danger   b. good luck   c. death

2. The pirate had a **black** heart that knew no mercy.

    a. warmth   b. love   c. evil

3. The young bride wore a **white** dress and veil.

    a. danger   b. fear   c. purity

4. "I'm not **yellow**," whispered Frederick as he stood on the high diving board. "I'm just cautious!"

    a. fear, cowardice   b. anger, hatred   c. gentleness, kindness

5. When Andrea saw her boyfriend with another girl, the **green**-eyed monster gripped her soul!

    a. love   b. jealousy   c. evil

SYNONYMS

In the sentences below, replace each *italicized* word with its *synonym* (word with a similar meaning) from the box.

immigrant	opportunities	peak	port

SYNONYM

1. The *newcomer* nervously answered questions at Ellis Island.

   _____

2. Millions of people from foreign lands sailed into the *harbor* of Ellis Island.

   _____

3. The *height* of immigration came between 1900 and 1909.

   _____

4. New arrivals hoped to find *chances* for a better life.

   _____

USING THE GRAPH

A *graph* is a chart that shows the changes taking place in something. Use information from the graph on page 87 to help you circle the answers to the following questions.

1. Between what years did the greatest number of immigrants come to America?

   a. 1840–1849   b. 1900–1909   c. 1920–1929

2. How many new Americans arrived between 1860 and 1869?

   a. two million   b. two billion   c. two thousand

3. What happened to the flow of immigrants after 1909?

   a. It stayed the same.   b. It lessened.   c. It increased.

4. How long is the time period covered by the graph?

   a. just over a century   b. less than a decade   c. one year

5. Which two words on the graph are synonyms?

   a. millions, years   b. newcomers, immigrants   c. America's, immigrants

Chief Joseph Speaks

In the late 1800s, Chief Joseph was head of the Nez Perce tribe. He became famous for his efforts to keep peace with the white settlers. But, again and again, Joseph saw the U.S. government break promises and ignore treaties. He was finally forced to go to war.

The government wanted to move the Nez Perce from the Wallowa Valley in Oregon to a reservation. Knowing that his tribe could never overpower the white soldiers, Joseph led a grueling retreat. Men, women, and children marched toward Canada. Joseph finally surrendered about 40 miles from the U.S.-Canadian border. He lived out his life on the Colville Indian Reservation in the state of Washington. Chief Joseph was an eloquent spokesman. These excerpts from his speeches echo his frustrations with broken promises.

Chief Joseph on war and peace:

For a short time we lived quietly. But this could not last . . . I labored hard to avoid trouble and bloodshed.

We gave up some of our country to the white men, thinking that then we could have peace. We were mistaken. . . .

Our young men are quick-tempered and I have had great trouble in keeping them from doing rash things. I have carried a heavy load on my back ever since I was a boy. I learned then that we were but few while the white men were many. . . . We had a small country. Their country was large. We were contented to let things remain as the Great Spirit Chief made them. They were not; and would change the mountains and rivers if they did not suit them.

Chief Joseph at his surrender in the Bear Paw Mountains, 1877:

I am tired of fighting. Our chiefs are killed. . . . My people—some of them have run away to the hills. . . . No one knows where they are—perhaps freezing to death. . . . Hear me, my chiefs, my heart is sick and sad. From where the sun now stands, I will fight no more forever.

WORD SEARCH

1. What eleven-letter noun from the reading means "public land set aside for special use"?

   _r_____

2. What twelve-letter plural noun from the reading means "feelings of disappointment, of being kept from what one wants"?

   _f_____

3. What eight-letter plural noun from the reading means "quoted sections of a speech, book, or article"?

   _e_____

SYNONYMS

• Write a letter to match each **boldface** word from the reading with its synonym.

1. _____ **grueling**   a. leader

2. _____ **eloquent**   b. exhausting

3. _____ **chief**   c. well-spoken

4. _____ **contented**   d. reflect

5. _____ **tribe**   e. clan

6. _____ **echo**   f. satisfied

• Now use each word from the first column in a sentence. Be sure the sentence makes the word's meaning clear.

1. _____

2. _____

3. _____

4. _____

5. _____

6. _____

ANTONYMS

Complete the puzzle with words from the reading. Clue words are *antonyms* (words with the opposite meaning) of the answer words.

ACROSS

1. rested
5. correct
7. peace
8. nomads

DOWN

2. mend
3. advance
4. heeds
6. cautious

COMPOUND WORDS

• Complete each sentence with a compound word from the reading. Combine the **boldface** words in the box to make the compound words.

blood	man	over	power	shed	spokes

1. The U.S. Army was large enough to_____ the Nez Perce warriors.

2. As a _____ for the Native Americans, Chief Joseph talked of his disappointment with the government's broken promises.

3. Joseph said he was tired of the _____ and sorrow of the battlefield.

• The compound word *spokesman* means a man who speaks for another or for a group.

4. What might you call a woman who speaks for others? _____

5. What might you call a person who speaks for others if you did not know the sex of the speaker? _____

The Monsoon

A *monsoon* is a seasonal wind that blows in over the land. Differences in temperature between land and sea air create the monsoon and direct its flow. In winter, a northeasterly monsoon blows dry winds. In summer, a monsoon travels from the southwest—from the cooler sea to the warmer land. The summer monsoon usually brings heavy rains to southern and southeastern Asia. It is a climatic event that farmers expect. Unusually strong monsoons, however, can bring too much rain. They can damage the economy by destroying crops and livestock.

It is the particular geography of land and sea that creates a monsoon. Ancient legends, however, provide their own reasons. This tale from Vietnam offers an interesting explanation of a monsoon.

Why the Monsoon Comes

Many men wanted to marry Princess Mi Nuong. One day, two suitors appeared. One was the Power of the Sea. The other was the Power of the Mountains.

"Fetch gifts for my daughter!" the emperor commanded. "Whoever returns first will be her husband."

The Power of the Sea gathered pearls, squid, and juicy crabs. The Power of the Mountains used magic to fill a giant chest with emeralds and diamonds. He returned to the palace first. Princess Mi Nuong married the Power of the Mountains.

The furious Power of the Sea sent wind and rain to the kingdom. Rivers flooded and many people perished. But the Power of the Mountain had taken the princess to his tallest peak—beyond the reach of the Power of the Sea.

The Power of the Sea saw that his efforts were useless, so he stopped the floods. But he remained angry. That is why the Power of the Sea still sends the monsoons to Vietnam every year.

WORD SEARCH

1. What six-letter noun from the reading means "a story handed down through the years"?

   _l_____

2. What seven-letter noun from the reading means "a system of producing and using wealth"?

   _e_____

SYNONYMS

Complete the puzzle with words from the reading. Clue words are *synonyms* (words with a similar meaning) of the answer words.

ACROSS

1. angry
4. interpretation
6. box

DOWN

2. octopus
3. died
5. castle

WORD FORMS

Write the indicated form of each **boldface** word. Hint: You will find the new word used in the reading.

1. **season** *(noun)* _____ *(adjective)*

2. **explain** *(verb)* _____ *(noun)*

3. **climate** *(noun)* _____ *(adjective)*

4. **magic** *(noun)* _____ *(adjective)*

5. **powerful** *(adjective)* _____ *(noun)*

USING CONTEXT CLUES

Use *context clues* in the reading to figure out the meaning of each **boldface** word below. Circle the letter of the best definition.

1. **suitor**
   a. a bag specially made for carrying suits
   b. a man who hopes to marry a certain woman
   c. an article of clothing that fits very well

2. **commanded**   a. questioned   b. suggested   c. ordered

3. **fetch**   a. go get   b. purchase   c. make by hand

4. **useless**
   a. without hope of success
   b. very successful
   c. extremely costly

CATEGORIES

Two of the words in each group have something in common. Underline the word that does *not* belong in each group.

1. squid   crabs   emeralds

2. wind   rain   mountains

3. emperor   monsoon   princess

4. flood   rain   drought

GEOGRAPHY MATCH

Write a letter to match each **boldface** word or words from the story with a geographical term. Write a letter beside the number. Use a dictionary if needed.

1. _____ **Asia**

2. _____ **Vietnam**

3. _____ **rain, wind**

4. _____ **emeralds, diamonds, crabs**

5. _____ **southern, northeasterly**

6. _____ **summer, winter**

a. climate

b. country

c. directions

d. seasons

e. continent

f. natural resources

King Tut's Tomb

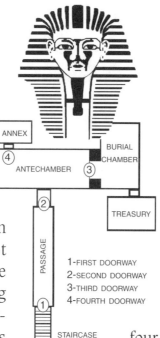

ANNEX

④ ANTECHAMBER ③

BURIAL CHAMBER

②

PASSAGE

TREASURY

1 - FIRST DOORWAY
2 - SECOND DOORWAY
3 - THIRD DOORWAY
4 - FOURTH DOORWAY

①

STAIRCASE

" . . . when we came to a golden shrine with doors closed and sealed, we realized we were to witness a spectacle such as no other man in our time had been privileged to see. . . ."

These words were written by British archeologist Howard Carter when he discovered the tomb of King Tutankhamen (toot-ahng-KAH-muhn). King Tut, as the pharaoh has been called, ruled Egypt more than 3,300 years ago. Because he became ruler at age nine, he is sometimes called "the boy king."

When he died at age 18, Tut's people followed the usual funeral custom for kings. They buried him in a giant tomb. Treasures and items of daily life were buried along with him. It was 1922, in the Valley of the Kings (the site of about 30 other tombs), that Carter and his party discovered entrance doors. Until then, they had been hidden by debris from a nearby digging.

What Carter saw inside the tomb amazed him. *"There, filling the entire area,"* he describes, *"stood an immense, yellow sarcophagus. . . . A gasp of wonderment escaped our lips, so gorgeous was the sight that met our eyes. A golden effigy of the young king . . ."*

The sarcophagus, or coffin, was carved with a lifelike gold mask of Tutankhamen. Inside it was the boy king's cloth-wrapped mummy. The four-room tomb also held more than 5,000 objects. There were carved chests, golden thrones, beds, clothing, and necklaces. There were chariots, bows and arrows, swords, shields, and trumpets. The ancient Egyptians believed in life after death. They buried the king's favorite toys and games along with practical objects he could use in the afterlife. Howard Carter had uncovered a rare prize—the only tomb of an Egyptian pharaoh ever to be found that was almost completely undamaged.

The treasures of King Tut's tomb have traveled to museums around the world. Most of the items are on permanent display in the Egyptian Museum in Cairo, Egypt.

WORD SEARCH

1. What twelve-letter noun from the reading means "a scientist who studies ancient times and people by digging up the remains of past civilizations"?   *a* _____

2. What eleven-letter noun from the reading means "a decorated coffin found in a tomb"?   *s* _____

SYNONYMS

Unscramble the words from the reading. Write each unscrambled word next to its *synonym* (word with a similar meaning).

MINEMES _____   **BMTO** _____

FIGYEF _____   **SIDYALP** _____

1. likeness _____   3. exhibition _____

2. vault _____   4. huge _____

WORD MEANINGS

Complete the puzzle with words from the reading. Clues are definitions of the answer words.

ACROSS

1. an open, two-wheeled cart drawn by horses

4. seldom found or seen; unusual

5. a brass horn that makes a loud, blaring sound

DOWN

2. a tomb or any spiritual place containing sacred items

3. useful in daily life

6. a cloth-wrapped body kept from rotting by the use of chemicals

WORD ROOTS

The Latin root *specto* means "look at." The word *inspect*, for example, means "to look at closely." Read the list of words containing *specto*. Then write a letter to match each word with its meaning. Use a dictionary if you need help.

1. _____ **spectacle**   a. a person who watches something

2. _____ **perspective**   b. an especially unusual sight

3. _____ **spectator**   c. eyeglasses

4. _____ **spectacles**   d. the way things look from a certain point
   (a pair of)

ANALOGIES

Analogies are statements of relationship. To come up with the missing word, you must figure out the relationship between the first two words. Then, complete each analogy with a word from the reading that shows the same relationship.

1. *Marriage* is to *wedding* as *death* is to _____.

2. *Ancient Russia* is to *czar* as *ancient Egypt* is to _____.

3. *Impossible* is to *possible* as _____ is to *damaged*.

4. *Timothy* is to *Tim* as *Tutankhamen* is to _____.

THINKING ABOUT THE READING

Circle a letter to show the answer to each question.

1. What would you find in Egypt's Valley of the Kings?

   a. tombs   b. the capital of government

2. Why is King Tut called the "boy king"?

   a. He ruled Egypt at   b. He was young-looking
      a very young age.   for his age.

3. Why was King Tut's tomb undiscovered for so long?

   a. Its entrance was hidden by dirt   b. It was much smaller
      and rocks from another digging.   than the other tombs.

Vocabulary Stretch

Get out your dictionary and thesaurus! The challenging activities in this lesson were especially chosen to stretch the limits of your vocabulary.

WORDS AND MEANINGS

Complete each definition with a word from the box. Check a dictionary if you need help.

metropolis	naturalized	traitor	truce	physical map	political map

1. A _____ is a large, important city.

2. A _____ is someone who does something to harm his or her own country, friends, or cause.

3. A _____ shows land elevations, such as hills, mountains, valleys, and deserts.

4. A _____ shows manmade boundaries, such as those of countries, states, counties, cities, and towns.

5. Both sides in a conflict call a _____ when they agree to a pause in the fighting.

6. When a person is _____, he or she is made a citizen.

USING CONTEXT CLUES

Use *context clues* to figure out which **boldface** word correctly completes each sentence. Underline the word.

1. The attraction of the sun and moon causes the ocean to have a high and low (**truce** / **tide**).

2. A drought, or long dry period, occurs when there is a lack of (**precipitation** / **metropolis**).

3. The ancient Egyptians, Aztecs, and Greeks all practiced (**polytheism** / **traitor**), worshipping gods of the sea, the sun, and other parts of nature.

4. A (**political** / **physical**) map of Europe as it was 100 years ago looks very different from a map of Europe today.

5. By examining each (**naturalized** / **artifact**) that a society left behind, historians discover how ancient people lived.

SYNONYMS

Complete the crossword puzzle with *synonyms* (words with a similar meaning) of the answer words.

ACROSS

2. turncoat
4. rainfall
5. cease-fire

DOWN

1. city
3. relic

LATIN WORD ROOTS

• The Latin word root *ars* means "art" or "skill in making something."

Which word from this lesson contains the root *ars*? _____

• Underline the word in each sentence below that contains the Latin root *ars*. Then write the meaning of the word. If necessary, use a dictionary for help.

1. The artist drew a lifelike picture of the children at play.

MEANING: _____

2. The artificial fruit looked delicious enough to eat.

MEANING: _____

3. The artisan invited visitors to his pottery workshop.

MEANING: _____

WORD PARTS

- When the word part *poly-* is part of a word, it usually means "much, many, or more than one."

  What word from the lesson begins with the word part *poly-*?   _____

- The following words all contain the word part *poly-*. Write a letter to match each word with its meaning. Use a dictionary if necessary.

  1. **polysyllable**   a. a musical piece having several separate melodies, such as a round

  2. **polygamist**   b. a word containing four or more syllables

  3. **polyglot**   c. someone who is married to more than one person at one time

  4. **polytechnic**   d. having to do with or teaching many scientific and technical subjects

  5. **polyphony**   e. speaking and understanding several languages

WORD FORMS

Add vowels *(a, e, i, o, u)* to complete the new form of each word.

1. polytheism *(noun)*   p__lyth__ __st__c *(adjective)*

2. traitor *(noun)*   tr__ __t__r__ __s *(adjective)*

3. metropolis *(noun)*   m__tr__p__l__t__n *(adjective)*

4. naturalized *(verb)*   n__t__r__l__z__t__ __n *(noun)*

5. tide *(noun)*   t__d__l *(adjective)*

REVIEW

Here's your chance to show what you know about the material you studied in this unit!

SENTENCE COMPLETION

Write words you learned in Unit 4 to complete the sentences.

1. An _____ is a scientist who studies people of the past by digging up the remains of their civilizations.

2. A _____ is a seasonal wind that can bring heavy summer rains.

3. Breaking horses and riding and roping cattle are events that take place at a _____.

4. The verbs *retreat* and *attack* are _____.

5. An _____ is someone who seeks a home in a new land.

6. To rewrite a quote in one's own words is to _____.

ANALOGIES

Remember that *analogies* are statements of relationship. Figure out the relationship between the first two words. Then complete each analogy with a word from the unit that shows the same relationship.

1. *Chief* is to *Native Americans* as _____ is to *ancient Egyptians.*

2. *Gas* is to *gasoline* as _____ is to *photograph.*

3. *Attack* is to *advance* as _____ is to *withdraw.*

4. *Richard* is to *Dick* as *formal name* is to _____.

5. *Suggest* is to *suggestion* as *immigrate* is to _____.

HIDDEN WORDS PUZZLE

• Find and circle the words in the hidden words puzzle. Words may go up, down, across, backward, or diagonally. Check off each word as you find it.

___ **FRONTIER**   ___ **TOMB**

___ **SEASONAL**   ___ **ALIAS**

___ **EXCERPTS**   ___ **FUNERAL**

___ **NEWCOMER**   ___ **TRIBE**

___ **PASSPORT**   ___ **ISLAND**

___ **RANCHER**   ___ **MUSEUM**

```
V S E A S O N A L G E
I T F J K J B U W R X
Y R U R C M A I D A C
M O N X O K E N T N E
U P E T D N A O U C R
S S R G N L T I G H P
E S A O S T R I B E T
U A L I A S Z O E R S
M P N E W C O M E R H
```

• Now use any **six** of the puzzle words in sentences of your own. Be sure that each of your sentences makes the word's meaning clear.

1. _____

2. _____

3. _____

4. _____

5. _____

6. _____

MULTIPLE MEANINGS

Explain the difference in meaning between these two phrases from the unit.

1. In the story of Nat Love, you read about Nat's talent for *breaking horses*. What does it mean to "break a horse"?

_____

2. In the story of Chief Joseph, you learned how the U.S. government *broke promises*. What does it mean to "break a promise"?

_____

MATCHING

Draw lines to match the names from the readings with the word that describes them.

1. _____ **Howard Carter**   a. cowboy

2. _____ **Tutankhamen**   b. pharaoh

3. _____ **Joseph**   c. archeologist

4. _____ **Nat Love**   d. suitor

5. _____ **Power of the Sea**   e. chief

MAKE IT TRUE

Each of the following statements is *false*. Change the *italicized* word to make the false statement into a *true* statement. Write the replacement word on the line.

1. The *winter* monsoon often brings heavy rains.   _____

2. "Pharaoh" is a word used for the *modern* kings of Egypt.   _____

3. The United States government wanted the Nez Perce to move to a *metropolis*.   _____

4. The words "entrance" and "exit" are *synonyms*.   _____

5. A story passed down over many years is called an *autobiography*.   _____

6. *Natives* are people who are making their home in a new land.   _____

7. Ellis Island was sometimes called the "Island of *Cheers*."   _____

END-OF-BOOK TEST

ELEMENTS OF VOCABULARY

- Complete the crossword puzzle with the *category name* suggested by the clue words. Answers are elements of vocabulary listed in the box below.

noun	verb	adjective	prefix	suffix
compound	synonyms	antonyms	homonyms	idiom

ACROSS

1. ancient, dusty, peaceful

3. *find greener pastures, left his mark*

4. peace / piece, rain / reign

6. citizen, country, declaration

8. wildlife, craftsperson, swampland

9. *-ion, -ist, -eer*

DOWN

1. fertile/barren, loyal/disloyal

2. rotate, surrender, elect

5. cemetery/graveyard, despot/dictator

7. *re-, un-, dis-*

- Now write an example of your own for each element of vocabulary. If possible, your examples should relate to the field of history or geography.

1. NOUN: _____

2. VERB: _____

3. ADJECTIVE: _____

4. COMPOUND WORD: _____

5. WORD WITH A PREFIX: _____

6. SYNONYMS: _____

7. ANTONYMS: _____

8. HOMONYMS: _____

9. IDIOM: _____

10. WORD WITH A SUFFIX: _____

GEOGRAPHICAL TERMS

- Match each word from the field of geography with its meaning. Write a letter by each number.

1. _____ **latitude**

2. _____ **longitude**

3. _____ **tropics**

4. _____ **drought**

5. _____ **coast**

a. land along the sea

b. the distance measured in degrees east and west of an imaginary line running from the North Pole to the South Pole

c. the distance north or south of the equator, measured in degrees

d. a mostly warm region of the Earth located between the Tropic of Cancer and the Tropic of Capricorn

e. a long dry spell

- Now underline the words that correctly complete each sentence about world geography.

1. The (North Pole / Arctic Circle) is the spot farthest north on the Earth.

2. The (time zone / South Pole) is the spot farthest south on the Earth.

3. The (equator / prime meridian) is an imaginary line that runs east and west around the center of the Earth.

4. A large stretch of flat land, often covered with grass, is called a (jungle / plain).

5. A (valley / volcano) is a low-lying area of land among hills.

ANTONYMS

Find and circle the hidden words in the puzzle. Words may go up, down, across, backward, or diagonally. Check off each word as you find it. When you have circled all the words, write each word next to its *antonym* (word that means the opposite).

___ ALLY   ___ CAPTURE

___ JUSTICE   ___ MAJORITY

___ NOBLE   ___ PENALTY

___ STEEP   ___ TOURIST

___ MODERN   ___ VICTORY

___ RETREAT   ___ FREEDOM

___ HOSTILE   ___ METROPOLIS

```
V  I  C  T  O  R  Y  H  W  M  J
O  T  P  E  N  A  L  T  Y  U  K
I  O  D  O  O  G  I  S  S  M  Y
H  U  F  B  B  U  C  T  W  R  T
O  R  A  R  L  V  I  Z  N  E  I
S  I  T  O  E  C  Y  M  R  T  R
T  S  S  T  E  E  P  L  E  R  O
I  T  O  R  J  A  D  G  D  E  J
L  I  A  L  L  Y  I  O  O  A  A
E  R  U  T  P  A  C  D  M  T  M
V  M  E  T  R  O  P  O  L  I  S
```

ANTONYMS:

1. opponent /_____

2. commoner / _____

3. bondage / _____

4. injustice / _____

5. ancient / _____

6. reward / _____

7. attack / _____

ANTONYMS:

8. village / _____

9. release / _____

10. friendly / _____

11. level / _____

12. defeat / _____

13. resident / _____

14. minority / _____

HOMONYMS

Homonyms are words that sound exactly alike but have different meanings and often different spellings. First figure out a homonym for each **boldface** word from the book. Then write a phrase, describing your homonym with two appropriate adjectives. The first one has been done for you.

	HOMONYM	PHRASE
1. **air**	*heir*	*the young, inexperienced heir*
2. **rain**		
3. **plane**		
4. **peace**		
5. **principal**		
6. **peek**		

WORDS IN CONTEXT

Underline the word from the unit that correctly completes each headline.

1. HEAVY PRECIPITATION BRINGS THREAT OF (FLOOD / DROUGHT)

2. U.S. AND MEXICO FORM TRADE (ASSASSIN / ALLIANCE)

3. PEACE (TREATY / TYRANT) ENDS CIVIL WAR

4. WATER POLLUTION THREATENS REGION'S (WILDLIFE / WARRIOR)

5. SOARING (TEMPERATURES / TRAITORS) SEND CITY-DWELLERS TO SHORELINES

6. FALLING ECONOMY BRINGS FEARS OF (DUST STORM / DEPRESSION)

7. CITIZENS OUST DICTATOR AND CALL FOR (CONFEDERACY / DEMOCRACY)

WORD LIST

Absentee
accompanied
accomplish
achievement
administration
adobe
advance
advisors
afterlife
age
aggressive
alias
alliance
allies
aloft
ambitious
amphitheater
anchor
ancient
angle
announcer
anthropology
aqueduct
arc
arch
archeologist
arctic
Arctic Circle
arrogant
article
artifact
artisan
aspect
assassin
assertive
assistant
atom bomb
attendant
autobiography
autonomy
awed
axis

Ballot
balmy

banned
banner
barren
battlefield
bay
belfry
beloved
bill
bitter
bizarre
blanketed
blaring
bloodshed
blotted
board
bonanza
borders
borne
boundary
brass
bronco
burro

Cactus
campaign
candidate
canines
canoes
canyon
capital
captive
capture
cargo
cart
cartographer
cartoon
cartoonist
castle
cautious
cease-fire
cemetery
centigrade
centimeter
centurion
century

ceremony
certain
channel
character
chariots
chemicals
chest
chief
chiseled
cipher
circumstances
citizen
city
city-state
civil
civil war
civilians
civilization
clan
climate
climatic
climatologist
coast
code
coffin
collapse
colonial
colonist
colony
column
combative
command
commoner
comparison
competition
comrade
conceived
concern
conduct
Confederacy
confident
conflict
conform
Congress
conquer

conquest
conquistador
conservation
conspire
constellation
constitution
contaminate
contented
contestants
contested
continent
contrast
controversial
cooperation
costly
country
county
courtyard
cowardly
cowboy
craftsperson
criticize
crops
cruise
crusade
culture
customs
czar

Daunting
dealt
debatable
debris
decaying
declaration
decoration
dedicate
defeat
defiance
degrees (°)
democracy
Democrat
demography
depression
desert

WORD LIST

designated
despite
despot
destruction
determination
devastation
dictator
disappointment
disciplined
dismaying
dispatch
displaying
distinct
document
dominion
donate
drafted
dreadful
drought
dust

Earth
east
echo
ecology
economy
education
effigy
election
elector
Electoral College
elevation
eloquent
embark
emblem
emerald
emerge
emperor
emphasis
empire
employment
enact
encourage
encrust
endangered
endear
energetic

enfeeble
engineer
engraved
enlist
enliven
enrich
entrance
entry
envisioned
epidemic
equality
equator
era
erect
err
erupt
especially
euphemism
event
exaggerated
examination
excerpts
exhausting
exhibition
expectations
explanation
explorers
extend

Factual
fascist
fashion
favors
fearsome
feat
features
federal
felines
fertile
festivities
fetch
fiercely
fled
flood
flourished
foes
foliage

forbidden
forecaster
foremost
forevermore
formal
forth
founding fathers
freedom
freight
frighten
frigid
frontier
frustrations
funeral
furious

Gasp
genius
genocide
geography
geology
globe
glorious
gorge
gorgeous
government
graph
grasp
grassland
gripped
grueling
guard
guidance
gulf

Harbor
harvesting
hearten
heed
heir
hero
historian
historical
hitched
homeless
horizontal
horsemanship

hostile
House of
  Representatives
humble
humorous
hysterical

Identification
immense
immigrants
impartiality
incumbent
indigenous
industrious
infantry
infertile
inherit
inspired
interpretation
invader
invasion
invest
island
isolated
isthmus

Jealousy
jerk
jigsaw
jungle
justice

King
kingdom

Labored
lake
landslide
lantern
latitude
laws
league
legend
legislation
liberty
likeness
livestock

llama
longitude
lowlands
loyalist
loyalty
luggage
lush

Maintain
majority
mangrove
mansion
marine
marsh
masses
measure
melody
memorial
memories
mend
mental
mercy
meridian
mesa
message
meteorologist
metropolis
midnight
Midwestern
migrant
migrate
migratory
militant
military
minority
misfortune
misleading
mission
model
modern
moisture
molten
monarchy
monsoon
monument
mortal
mountain

mummified
mummy
museum
mustang
mystical

Nation
national park
native
natural
naturalized
Nazi
neighbor
neutrality
newcomers
noble
nobleman
nomad
nominate
north
North Pole
noticeable

Obedience
objects
ocean
octopus
official
opponent
oppose
opposition
oppress
order
ore
origin
oust
outcome
overpower
overseas
overthrow
overwhelming

Pacifist
palace
parallel
parched
passages

passport
pastures
patriot
peace
peacekeeper
peak
penalty
perched
peril
perish
perspective
pharaoh
phenomenon
philosophy
physical map
pillar
pioneers
plague
plain
platoon
plot
political map
politics
pollutants
pollute
polygamist
polyglot
polyphony
polysyllable
polytechnic
polytheism
popular
popularize
population
port
porter
pottery
practical
prairie
precipitation
preserved
president
prime meridian
primitive
principle
privileges
promote

promptly
propaganda
proposal
proposition
prospered
prosperity
psychology
punished
purchase
purity

Quality
quarrel
quick-tempered
quoted

Raft
ranch
rank
rapid
rare
rash
react
realized
realm
reassigned
recession
referred
reforms
regent
region
reign
relay
relic
relocated
remote
representative
Republican
resent
reservation
residence
resident
resign
resolve
resources
retreat
retrieve

revolt
revolution
revolutionary
ringing
river
rodeo
role
rotate
rotation
rotting
route

Sacred
sarcophagus
satirical
satirize
scarlet
scheme
science
scout
sculpted
season
seasonal
secluded
seldom
sensational
sentry
serfs
servant
settle
shack
shattered
shields
shifty
showmanship
shrewd
shrine
siege
sightseer
site
sketch
slave
slopes
society
soldier
sole
sorrow

sought
south
South Pole
souvenir
species
spectacle
spectacular
spectator
speech
spiritual
spokesman
spongy
squid
staggering
standard
state
statue
stature
steed
steep
steeple
stock
stream
structures
stubborn
stylist
subjects
submarine
subordinate
suburb
suitors
sun
superlative
supremacy
surface
surrender
swamp
swift
symbol
symbolize

Tackled
tales
tank
task
temper
temperate

temperature
temple
term
terrain
territories
thaw
thrived
throne
thus
tide
tills
time line
time zone
title
tomb
topsoil
torrid
tourist
tragic
traitor
traits
traveler
treasures
treaty
trench
tribal
tribe
triumph
troops
Tropic of Cancer
Tropic of Capricorn
tropical
tropics
truce
trumpets
tunnel
turmoil
turncoat
twinkled
tyranny
tyrant

Unconstitutional
unearth
union
unique
unite

unjust
unlikely
unrealistic
uproar

Vain
valley
varied
vast
vault
vehicle
Venn diagram
vertical
veteran
victim
victorious
victory
village
volcanic
vote

Warfare
warn
warrior
waterway
wealth
weapon
weather
welfare
west
White House
wilderness
wildlife
windswept
withdrawal
witness
wonderment
workmanship
workshop
worship

Yield
youth

Zodiac
zone